# 1. Introduction

Whether market participants view certain financial firms as likely to receive government support in future times of stress is an open empirical question. Understanding and quantifying such expectations is relevant since such expectations could give financial firms perceived as too-important-to-fail an advantage in doing business over other firms due to their lower perceived risk. In addition, expectations of implicit government guarantees could further weaken financial stability by lowering the incentives of investors and other stakeholders to monitor firms with perceived implicit guarantees or by increasing risk-taking by financial firms (e.g., Flannery and Sorescu (1996), Iyer, Puri, and Ryan (2013), and Gropp, Hakenes, and Schnabel (2011)).

A common approach to measuring expectations of implicit government guarantees is to test whether the borrowing costs of firms that investors may view as being more likely to receive government support, typically measured by firms size, are lower than those of other firms. Since the bonds of such "too-big-to-fail" firms should be less likely to default, investors should demand lower returns on these bonds, all else equal.

However, even in the absence of a government guarantee, large financial firms may borrow more cheaply than small financial firms. Relating size to otherwise unobserved risk factors is common in asset pricing literature (e.g. Chan and Chen (1988)), and size is often used as a control variable in studies of credit spreads. To evidence a government guarantee, size-related funding cost differentials should seem unusual in banking relative to industries not subject to a guarantee (e.g., Kroszner (2013)).

In this paper, we show that borrowing cost differentials between large and small financial firms are not unusually large relative to differentials we observe in other industries. We compare size-related borrowing cost differentials across industries to determine how size affects the cost of debt financing. Our methodology allows for industry-specific size effects in borrowing costs and controls for firm-specific default risk.

While we find that large financial firms borrow more cheaply than small financial firms, the financial industry does not seem unusual in terms of this size effect. However, we do find evidence that financial firms as a group, particularly commercial and investment banking firms, have lower average costs of borrowing compared with similar firms in other industries, particularly prior to the financial crisis. This suggests that financial firms, taken as a whole, may be more likely to be viewed as less risky compared to firms in other industries, perhaps due to investor views that the government is more likely to intervene in this industry in times of stress.[1]

Specifically, we examine the quarterly credit default swap (CDS) and bond spreads for financial and non-financial firms over the period 2004 to 2013 and how these spreads relate to firm size, controlling for a number of factors including firm-specific risk. We find that larger

---

[1]This finding is consistent with a recent paper by Kelly, Lustig, and Van Nieuwerburgh (2011) who find using option data that the financial industry, as a whole, is perceived as less risky.

2

firms have lower spreads in most industries. The negative relation between firm size and spread is larger in many non-financial industries than it is in financial industries, especially prior to the financial crisis. During the financial crisis, the negative relation between firm size and spreads became weaker across all non-financial industries and slightly stronger for commercial and investment banking firms. However, following the financial crisis, this pattern has reversed.

To understand the reasons behind the size effect in CDS and bond spreads, we explore explanations related to differences in liquidity and recovery rates. Greater liquidity could lower the cost of borrowing for larger firms. In addition, economies of scale in debt issuance could advantage larger or more familiar issuers. Similarly, recovery rate advantages related to issuer size could lead to lower borrowing costs for equivalent levels of default risk. When we control for these factors, we find that liquidity affects borrowing costs, but we still find size-related borrowing cost advantages in most industries outside the financial crisis. We also find preliminary evidence of a relationship between recovery rates and size, but inter-industry analysis suggests this relationship is driven by a small number of non-financial industries.

Our results suggest that size-related differences in the cost of borrowing amongst financial firms do not necessarily reflect investors' expectations of a higher likelihood of government support for the larger firms. If anything, our results suggest that investors in the bonds and CDS of financial firms may view firms in these industries as overall less risky compared to firms in non-financial industries, and that this was especially true prior to the financial crisis. Whether or not any lower overall perceived risk is due to investor expectations of government support or due to other factors is an open empirical question.

Our study is unique on several dimensions, allowing us to generate new results and insights into the literature on measuring implicit government guarantees. First, by using CDS data, in addition to bond data, we are more able to make an "apples-to-apples" comparison between firms of different sizes and in different industries. Examining spreads on standard CDS instruments eliminates the need to control for a range of security characteristics, as must be done when examining bond spreads or deposit rates CDS spreads should in theory be equal to the spread of the underlying corporate bond since the CDS acts as insurance against the event of default of the underlying bond, and in practice CDS and corporate bond spreads are highly correlated (e.g., Houweling and Vorst (2005))[2] Thus, examining CDS spreads, in addition to directly examining corporate bond spreads, reduces the likelihood that observed differences in borrowing costs are driven by differences in characteristics of the underlying bonds rather than differences in firm characteristics and allows us to analyze a large sample of firms.

Second, the set of firms for which there are both CDS and public bonds trading lie towards the top of the firm-size distribution, allowing a more meaningful comparison of borrowing

---

[2]Only a handful of other studies in the implicit government guarantee literature examine CDS spreads Li and Zhang (2011) examine CDS spreads of financial firms only. Demirguc-Kunt and Huizinga (2013) examine CDS spreads and equity prices in an international sample of banks and find that in some countries banks may have become "too-big-to-save" rather than "too-big-to-fail".

4

costs by firm size since comparing borrowing costs of very small banks to very large banks may shed less light on any "too-big-to-fail" subsidy than comparing the largest banks to large, but still smaller, banks.

Third, since we conduct our exercise across all industries, we are able to more directly control for other differences between small and large firms that may cause their costs of borrowing to differ besides implicit government guarantees (e.g., Kroszner (2013)). We examine a number of different firm size variables to account for differences in the underlying firm size distributions across industries.

Our study is most similar to studies which explicitly examine the costs of debt between financial firms, such as Acharya, Anginer, and Warburton (2013) and Santos (2014), who examine differences in bond spreads between large and small financial firms, and Jacewitz and Pogach (2012) and Bassett (2014), who examine differences in the cost of deposits by large and small banks. We study differences in CDS and bond spreads between large and small banks, as well as large and small financial firms and non-financial firms more generally, but adopt a more comprehensive approach to econometrically modelling credit spreads as a function of firm industry and sizein a large sample of firms. Several studies have examined differences in the size sensitivity of bond spreads of financial firms relative to non-financial firms. However, these studies either group non-financial firms together in to one broad category over many years (e.g., Acharya et al. (2013)) or are limited to small samples (e.g.,

Santos (2014)).

The remainder of the paper proceeds as follows. Section 2 discusses related literature on why we may observe firm-size-related differential costs of borrowing. Section 3 describes the data. Section 4 presents our main results. Section 5 explores the roles of liquidity and recovery rates in explaining the observed size effects in credit spreads. Section 6 discusses the economic magnitudes of estimates. Section 7 concludes.

## 2. Related literature

In this section, we briefly review the literature which discusses why larger financial firms may have borrowing costs, how these explanations have been examined in other studies, and how they are examined in our setting.

### 2.1. Size anomaly

The strong empirical negative relation of firm size on equity and debt returns has long been recognized (e.g. Banz (1981), Fama and French (1992)). While the negative empirical relation between size and returns is typically cited as evidence of mis-specification of the underlying asset pricing model or mis-measurement of the model's risk factors (e.g., Berk (1995), Gandhi and Lustig (forthcoming)), it is clear that firm size is correlated in most cases with factors or omitted variables indicating lower risk.

We also find that firm size is strongly negatively correlated with the cost of borrowing, as measured by CDS and bond spreads. This is true across most industries. Thus, our analysis is consistent with the findings in the "size anomaly" literature. We attempt to parse out the components of the size effect in our data, in particular, by measuring the liquidity of a firm's CDS and bonds and the expected recovery rates on the bonds, as we discuss below. Still after controlling for these factors, we find that size is still negatively correlated with CDS and bond spreads in both financial and non-financial firms.

## 2.2. Too-big-to-fail (TBTF) subsidy

One possible explanation of the size effect in borrowing costs and expected returns in financial firms is that larger financial firms may be perceived by investors as more likely to be bailed out by governments in the event of distress. This explanation has received a lot of study recently in light of the financial crisis of 2008 and 2009 and the widely publicized government support received by several large financial institutions.

Approaches to estimating any TBTF subsidy vary. Many focus on estimating the difference in borrowing costs between large and small banks controlling for observable characteristics of the banks and borrowing instruments. For example Acharya et al. (2013), Santos (2014), and GAO (2014) focus on relating bond spreads to financial firm size. Tsesmelidakis and Merton (2013) use bond data and a structural model to form estimates of implicit government guarantees. Jacewitz and Pogach (2012), O'Hara and Shaw (1990), and Bassett (2014) focus on differences in bank deposit rates of large and small banks. Araten and Turner (2013) examine the cost of funding for a variety of funding sources. Ueda and Weder di Mauro (2013) focuses on differences in credit ratings of large and small banks. Others such as Brewer III and Jagtiani (2013) estimate how much financial firms pay to acquire other firms to reach a certain size threshold. Gandhi and Lustig (forthcoming) use equity returns to show that investors may perceive the largest banks as being more likely to receive government support in times of stress. Kelly et al. (2011) present evidence using options data that investors place a higher probability on the financial sector receiving government support as a whole compared to individual financial firms.

Several recent studies have adopted this empirical approach and have concluded that the value of an implicit guarantee to large financial firms can be sizable (e.g., Acharya et al. (2013), Tsesmelidakis and Merton (2013), Ueda and Weder di Mauro (2013), Araten and Turner (2013), Noss and Sowerbutts (2012), Jacewitz and Pogach (2012), Penas and Unal (2004)).

Many of these studies find evidence of a TBTF subsidy during the financial crisis, but also in the periods before and after. Given the size anomaly literature discussed above, however, it is difficult to say with certainty that correlations between size or other measures of the likelihood of government support do not proxy for other factors, which we discuss below.[3]

---

[3]For a recent discussion of some of the challenges to estimating implicit government guarantees, see Kroszner (2013).

## 2.3. Economies of scale

Larger firms may be more efficient and have lower costs or be less likely to fail relative to smaller firms. Indeed recent studies, such as Hughes, Mester, and Moon (2001), Wheelock and Wilson (2012), Hughes and Mester (2013), and Kovner, Vickery, and Zhou (2014), find evidence of economies of scale in the banking industry. To the extent that firm size and associated economies of scale in production lead to lower bankruptcy risk, then size should be negatively related to the cost of borrowing. If measures of probability of default accurately capture the impact of production economies of scale, then size may be less likely to proxy for economies of scale in pricing regressions.

A second form of economies of scale may be in the frequency with which a firm issues bonds. If firms issue debt more frequently there may be lower transactions costs and greater transparency surrounding the debt issues, leading to lower spreads and costs of borrowing. We form a variables, which we discuss below, to measure potential economies of scale in debt securities issuance.

## 2.4. Liquidity

Securities issued by larger firms may be more liquid, leading to lower spreads. Dick-Nielsen, Feldhütter, and Lando (2012) find evidence that bonds experienced greater spreads due to illiquidity during the financial crisis, suggesting that to the extent size serves as a proxy for liquidity risk, that lower spreads on larger firms might be partially driven by liquidity. We form two variables meant to capture the degree of liquidity in firms CDS and bond trading markets, which we discuss in Section 3.

## 2.5. Recovery rates

Finally the cost of borrowing may be lower if expected recovery rates in the event of default are higher (e.g., Doshi (2011) and Acharya, Bharath, and Srinivasan (2007), Carey and Gordy (2009)). We relate firm size to expected recovery rates in the event of a bond default to parse out the extent to which the size sensitivity of bond and CDS spreads may be driven by differences in expected recovery rates.

As we discuss below, we attemp to control for these factors in addition to firm size. In addition, and most importantly, we compare the size effect across industries over time to assess whether the size effect seems unique or unusual to financial firms.

# 3.  Data

We analyze quarterly CDS data (2004Q1-2013Q2) for a broad sample of U.S. firms. We collect data on credit default swap (CDS) spreads from Markit and quarterly balance sheet information from Standard & Poor's Financial Services LLC Compustat via Wharton Research Data Services (Compustat). We restrict attention to five-year non-government CDS spreads from Markit for senior unsecured debt denominated in U.S. dollars with a modified restructuring documentation clause. This restriction ensures that CDS spreads for different firms are comparable in terms of debt type and maturity. For each quarterly observation, we choose the last available CDS spread. Our CDS sample includes all firms for which these data are available. The CDS sample contains 17,486 observations for 665 unique firms.

We rely on estimates of firms' default risk based on five-year EDF from Moody's Analytics, CreditEdge. Moody's calculates the five-year EDF using a structural model based on stock valuations, balance sheet information, and realized asset volatility. The CreditEdge model first calculates a theoretical default risk using a structural model similar to Merton (1974). Moody's calculates the EDF by comparing the distribution of theoretical default risk to subsequent realized defaults. The five-year EDF calculations do not rely on bond yields or CDS spreads.

We complement CDS data with data on bond trading from Financial Industry Regulatory Authority: Trade Reporting and Compliance Engine (TRACE). We drop observations for which reported yields exceed 25% as they likely include data errors. We keep trades exceeding $10 million. For each bond on each day, we record the median reported yield. We merge the bond data with Moody's CreditEdge to obtain the EDF on the same day as the bond trade.

We obtain data on bond characteristics from Mergent's Fixed Income Securities Database (FISD) and Securities Data Corporation (SDC) Platinum. We exclude bonds with floating interest rates, callable bonds, convertible bonds, and issues flagged as preferred stock. For each bond, we subtract the yield on zero-coupon U.S. treasury bonds with the same maturity to obtain the yield spread.[4] We retain the last quarterly observation for each matched bond. For issuers with multiple bonds, we retain the bond with maturity closest to 5 years. The bond trading sample contains 16,006 observations for 319 unique firms. The difference in CDS and bond sample sizes is due to the requirement that bonds not have floating interest rate, be callabe or convertible, whereas CDS written on such bonds are included. In addition, some bond sample observations are dropped because we cannot match them to the FSID or SDC data.

We classify firms into industries using their primary SIC code. Non-financial firms are classified according to the Fama-French 12 Industry classifications. Financial firms (which fall under the "Money" Fama-French 12 industry classification) are further classified into banking, trading, and other financial based on the Fama-French 48 industry classifications.[5] We end up with fourteen industries: Banking, business equipment, chemicals, consumer durables, consumer non-durables, energy, health care, manufacturing, other financial, other non-financial, shops, telecommunications, trading, and utilities. Typically banking consists of commercial banks, trading consists of investment banks and brokerages, and other financial consists of insurance companies.

To measure the effect of liquidity or economies of scale in debt issuance, we analyze two variables designed to reflect liquidity benefits for particular firms. We measure CDS liquidity

---

[4]We add a fixed quantity, one thousand basis points, before taking the log to include bonds with negative yield spreads in the regression analysis.

[5]A detailed mapping from SIC codes to Fama-French industry classifications is available at Ken French's web page: http://mba.tuck.dartmouth.edu/pages/faculty/ken.french/.

using Markit data. *Depth* measures the daily number of contributor prices used to calculate the 5 year CDS spread. It is essentially a measure of the amount of trading in comparable CDS contracts. We measure economies of scale in debt issuance using *Raise*, the amount of debt (in millions) issued by a firm over the previous five years according to the Mergent FSID database. Appendix Table A.1 in the provides details on the definition of each variable we form and the associated data source.

Tables 1 presents means for the analysis variables in the CDS sample by firm industry. CDS spreads range in value from 401 (for Consumer Durables) to 119 (for Utilities). The financial industries have mean spreads that range from 178 for Banking to 269 for Other Financial. Banking firms have the largest mean size at 12.1 in log units, which translates to 18 billion dollars. Banking firms are also the most highly levered, given their unique capital structure consisting of deposits as well as bonds and equity. Trading firms have leverage ratios in line with Telecommunications and Utilities firms at around 47 percent. Half of banking firms in the sample lie in the top 5 percent of the size distribution compared to 20 percent of trading firms. These percentage are in line with other industries.

Table 2 presents mean statistics for the bond sample and shows similar patterns. Variation of these statistics over time periods we analyze is summarized in the Appendix Tables A.2 and A.3. Both spreads and EDFs are quite low for banking firms prior to the crisis (2004Q1:2008Q2) compared to other industries and then spike during the crisis period

(2008Q3:2009Q2). Banking firm spreads and EDFs fall in the post-crisis period (2009Q3:2013Q2).

Table 3 presents the number of unique firms by industry and year for CDS (Panel A), and bond (Panel B) samples. There are a fairly constant number of firms in each year in both samples.

# 4. Results

We begin our inter-industry analysis of the effect of size on borrowing costs by focusing on CDS spreads. To this end, we focus generally on the coefficient on size in credit spread regressions featuring various controls. We begin by analyzing all industries together and measuring the average impact of size on credit spreads for all borrowers across several specifications. After presenting aggregate results, we consider models that allow size-related coefficients to vary across industries, and interpret variation in these coefficients as industry-specific size effects. This approach is based on the premise that the existence of material bailout subsidies for financial borrowers would lead to rejection of the null hypothesis that the size effect for financial borrowers is no larger than that for borrowers in other industries. We also consider several size variables and specifications to account for the fact that industries have different underlying size distibutions.

## 4.1. The size effect for banking and trading financial firms

We begin by examining the raw differences in borrowing costs and the size effect for

the two largest categories of financial firms - banking and trading - compared to all other

industries. We do this to set a baseline and to compare our results to other studies that

compare funding costs of financial firms to those of non-financial firms. In Table 4, we

present regression results based on estimating a baseline model with two financial industry

indicator variables:

$$
\begin{aligned}
Log(Spread)_{i,j,t} =& \beta_1 LogSize_{i,t} + \beta_2 EDF_{i,t} + \beta_3 EDF_{i,t}^2 \\
&+ \beta_4 * I_{Banking} * EDF_{i,t} + \beta_5 * I_{Banking} * EDF_{i,t}^2 + \beta_6 * I_{Banking} * LogSize_{i,t} \\
&+ \beta_7 * I_{Trading} * EDF_{i,t} + \beta_8 * I_{Trading} * EDF_{i,t}^2 + \beta_9 * I_{Trading} * LogSize_{i,t} \\
&+ Industry_j FE + Quarter_t FE + \varepsilon_{i,t}
\end{aligned}
$$

$$(1)$$

where $i$ indexes firms, $j$ indexes industries, $t$ indexes time (quarter), and $I_{Banking}$ and $I_{Trading}$

represent indicators for banking and trading industries. $Log(Spread)$ is the log of the 5-year

CDS spread. Our primary measure of size, $LogSize$, is the logarithm of book assets. We

include both $EDF$ and its square in specifications starting in Column 2 to capture nonlinear

default risk-related effects. We also estimate the model in Column 3 (which corresponds

directly to Equation 1) for pre-crisis, crisis, and post-crisis sub-samples (Columns 4 to 6).

In Table 4, we highlight banking and trading industry fixed effects, as well as interactions of banking and trading indicator variables with default risk and size measures. The coefficient on size (measured by log assets) is negative and significant across all specifications except that for the crisis subsample (Column 5). This can be interpreted as an average effect: larger firms generally borrow more cheaply than smaller firms. This result remains even after controlling for non-linear effects of credit risk.

Results for banking and trading industries here are surprising: aside from the crisis period, the fixed effects for each industry are negative, but each industry's interaction with *LogSize* is positive. These results suggest that generally, banking and trading exhibit lower overall borrowing costs, but do not enjoy size-related borrowing cost advantages relative to the set of other industries.[6]

During the crisis period, these patterns reverse, with positive coefficients on financial industry indicator variables and negative coefficients on their interaction with size. We don't find a negative result on *LogSize* during the crisis, but the result for the interaction of the size and indicators for banking and trading are negative during the crisis. These crisis results are significant for Trading firms but not for Banking firms. This suggests some evidence of financial industry size-related borrowing advantages during the financial crisis, which we will examine in more detail later.

To complement our CDS-based analysis, we examine corporate bond trade yield spreads

---

[6]These estimates of the size effect stand in contrast to estimates in other papers, such as Acharya et al. (2013)) The lower overall CDS spreads of banking firms prior to the financial crisis is consistent with a recent study by Kelly et al. (2011) who find that options price lower overall risk in the financial industry.

using bond trading data in TRACE. We estimate the following equation:

$$Log(Spread)_{i,j,t} = \beta_1 LogSize_{i,t} + \beta_2 EDF_{i,t} + \beta_3 EDF_{i,t}^2$$

$$+ \beta_4 * I_{Banking} * EDF_{i,t} + \beta_5 * I_{Banking} * EDF_{i,t}^2 + \beta_6 * I_{Banking} * LogSize_{i,t}$$

$$+ \beta_7 * I_{Trading} * EDF_{i,t} + \beta_8 * I_{Trading} * EDF_{i,t}^2 + \beta_9 * I_{Trading} * LogSize_{i,t}$$

$$+ \beta_{10} Maturity_{i,t} + Industy_j FE + Quarter_t FE + \varepsilon_{i,t}$$

$$(2)$$

We present analogous results based on estimating Equation 2 in Table 5. The model we estimate is is similar to that in Equation 1 but controls for bond maturity. Results from bond data present some similar patterns compared with CDS results: larger firms generally enjoy borrowing cost advantages, as do banking and trading firms. Banking and trading firms have lower overall average costs outside the crisis (as exhibited by the coefficients on industry indicator variables). However, size-industry interactions are actually positive and significant for these firms, suggesting little evidence of unusual size-related financial industry borrowing cost advantages. The coefficient on size is negative and significant across specifications, and positive coefficients on size-industry interactions for banking and trading go from positive to insignificant during the crisis. During the financial crisis period (Column 5 of Table 5), we also see different results here than for CDS data we analyze in Table 4: the size coefficient remains negative and significant, and industry fixed effects for banking and trading, as well as corresponding industry-size interactions, are statistically insignificant.

## 4.2. The size effect across industries

While results in Tables 4 and 5 present suggestive evidence, they also involve comparisons of industry-size effects for two financial industries with a set of all other industries. To allow for comparison of such effects in financial industries with analogous effects in other individual industries, we further consider estimating effects separately for each industry. We augment the regression in Equation 1 to include size-related and default-risk effects for each individual industry, and estimate the following baseline model:

$$Log(Spread)_{i,j,t} = \sum_j \beta_{1,j} LogSize_{i,t} + \sum_j \beta_{2,j} EDF_{i,t} + \sum_j \beta_{3,j} EDF_{i,t}^2$$
$$+ Industy_j FE + Quarter_t FE + \varepsilon_{i,t} \tag{3}$$

Table 6, Column 1, displays full-sample estimates of $\beta_{1,j}$, the coefficient on size-industry interactions for each industry. Columns 2, 3 and 4 estimate the same specification across time periods. This table illustrates the primary observation in this paper: the size effect in financial firm borrowing costs is not unusual. Here, size-industry interactions are generally negative for financial firms, as we might expect. However, the magnitude of these negative effects is not unusually high in financial industries relative to analogous estimates for effects in other industries. In fact, it is not even highest in financial industries, as we find larger (negative) effects for industries like business equipment and energy. For several industries not considered bailout candidates, the size effect is larger than it is for financial industries. For example, the banking industry has coefficients on size of -0.003 in the Pre-Crisis period and -0.24 in the Post-Crisis period; while the Shops industry has size coefficients of -0.045 and -0.030 and the Business Equipment industry has size coefficients of -0.032 and -0.028.

There is a notable exception: during the financial crisis, the size effect is higher for banking and trading firms than for firms in other industries. The crisis affects banking and trading differently than other industries. Most industries see the magnitude of the size effect decrease during the financial crisis, whereas banking and trading see the size effect increase to -0.057 and -0.036, respectively. However the size effect for those two industries decreases in the post-crisis period. The evidence is consistent with both expectations and actualizations of government support for banking and trading during the crisis, but disappearing before and after.

The consumer durables industry seems anomalous in several specifications, with positive size effects. These results emerge because of the lower number of firms in this industry, combined with distress or near-distress in larger firms (auto manufacturers) during much of the sample period. Consumer durables exhibits a significant positive size effect, indicating that larger firms borrow at higher rates.

## 4.3. Nonlinear size effect

Because implicit guarantees may only apply to the largest firms, and because the underlying firm size distribution varies across industries, we also consider a specification that includes both our size measure (logarithm of book assets) and an indicator variable for firms above the $95^{th}$ percentile for size in their industry (as measured by all firms in the industry within the Compustat universe of firms). This allows estimation of both discrete and continuous size effects. We estimate the following specification for pre-crisis, crisis, and post-crisis periods:

$$Log(Spread)_{i,j,t} = \sum_{j} \beta_{1,j} LogSize_{i,t} + \sum_{j} \beta_{2,j} Size95_{i,t} + \sum_{j} \beta_{3,j} EDF_{i,t} + \sum_{j} \beta_{4,j} EDF_{i,t}^2$$
$$+ Industy_j FE + Quarter_t FE + \varepsilon_{i,t}$$

$$(4)$$

Results, presented in Table 7, illustrate a consistent pattern: the importance of size for financial firms' borrowing costs does not appear unusually large relative to that for other industries. Here, we estimate a discrete effect that enters for the largest firms, measured by $\beta_{2,j}$ in Equation 4 for each industry. Our results suggest that while there may be borrowing cost advantages for the largest firms, they are not highest for financial firms, as other firms exhibit higher size-related borrowing cost advantages for the overall size effect (coefficient on $LogSize$) and for a nonlinear large firm effect (coefficient on $Size95$).

While they are not unusually high or highest across industries, we do find some evidence of high size-related borrowing cost advantages for the largest 5% of banking firms both overall and during the financial crisis, but the coefficients are statistically insignificant.

## 4.4. Results with bond data

In Tables 8 and 9, we present results of estimating Equations 3 (size effect across industries) and 4 (nonlinear size effect) for the bond sample. These results illustrate a similar pattern: size-based borrowing cost advantages for financial firms are not unusually large compared with similar effects in other industries. Results from Table 8 largely mirror those from Table 6: analyzing both samples suggest the size effect within financial firms is largest in the other financial category, although they are still not largest among all industries.

Similarly, results using bond data presented in Table 9 are similar to those using CDS data in Table 7. The continuous and discrete size effects are both higher in a number of non-financial industries than they are in the financial industries. The bond sample presents stronger evidence of a full-sample nonlinear size effect in banking, although this effect does not appear in the post-crisis sample. During this period, by contrast, we find that the largest trading firms experience significant cost disadvantages in the presence of size-based borrowing advantages for the industry overall.

## 4.5. Robustness to size variable

While we focus primarily on the logarithm of book assets, a commonly used size measure, we also examine results for alternative measures: the $Size95$ variable described in the previous section, and a standardized version of log total assets, which measures size in units of standard deviation from the mean log of total assets for all other Compustat firms in the same industry. The standardized size measure allows another way of adjusting for the fact that the underlying firm size distributions across industries varies. Analysis with standardized size variables is presented in Appendix Tables A.4 (for the CDS sample) and A.5 (for the bond sample).

We also restrict our analysis to the set of firms with both non-missing CDS and bond data, reported in Appendix Table A.6, and find that our main results are robust.

To aid in the comparison of the esimated size effects by size variable, we graph he coefficients for pre-crisis, crisis and post-crisis size-industry interaction terms are illustrated for CDS data in Figures 1 through 3 and for bond data in Figures 4 through 6. Since the coefficients on different size measures are in different units, we instead plot normalized size coefficients which are comparable across different size measures. We normalize the size coefficients by subtracting the mean coefficient for a given specification and dividing by the standard error of the coefficients.

The figures illustrate that both the pre- and post-crisis size effects for financial firms are similar to those for other industries. These results generally support our conclusions. For the banking industry during the crisis and for other financial firms post-crisis, the estimated coefficient on the industry interaction with $Size95$ is higher than it is for other industries.

## 4.6. Robustness to default risk specification

In the previous analysis, we relied on the EDF measure to proxy for firm-speciffic default risk. It is possible that EDF may not accurately capture non-government support default risk if the EDF reflects lower default probability due to higher equity values that may result from implicit guarantees of financial firms' bonds. If this is the case, then EDF could be biased downward, reflecting the implicit government guarantee.

Thus, we also estimate our baseline regressions using alternative measures of default risk, namely firm leverage and credit rating. This analysis with alternative default risk specifications based on leverage and credit ratings are presented in Appendix Tables A.7 (for the CDS sample) and A.8 (for the bond sample). Our results our robust to these alternative default risk specifications. In particular, we only observe larger than average size effects for the financial industries during the crisis period.

# 5.  Explaining the size effect

Having documented the size effect under using a number of size variables and specifications, we proceed to examine possible explanations. We consider two candidates: liquidity and recovery rates. If larger firms enjoy economies of scale in debt issuance, their borrowing costs could be systematically lower. Similarly, higher expected recovery rates could lead to lower borrowing costs holding the probability of default constant.

## 5.1. Liquidity

In order to test the hypothesis that larger firms have lower funding costs due to more liquid markets for their securities or economies of scale from seasoned issuance, we examine the impact of adding additional control variables. *Raise* is debt issuance over the past five years and *Depth* measures the amount of trading in a particular CDS contract. See Section 3 for a full explanation of these variables. We interact these additional variables by industry to capture industry-specific effects. To measure the effect of our liquidity variables, we estimate the following equation:

$$Log(Spread)_{i,j,t} = \sum_j \beta_{1,j} LogSize_{i,t} + \sum_j \beta_{2,j} Log(Raise_{i,t}) + \sum_j \beta_{3,j} Depth_{i,t} +$$
$$\sum_j \beta_{4,j} EDF_{i,t} + \sum_j \beta_{5,j} EDF_{i,t}^2 + Industy_j FE + Quarter_t FE + \varepsilon_{i,t} \tag{5}$$

Table 10 presents results of estimating Equation 5 for the liquidity-augmented specification. The main result remains: the size effect in financial industries is similar to the size effect in non-financial industries outside of the financial crisis, and in fact size effects are larger in several industries than in any financial industry. During the financial crisis, trading firms appear to enjoy unusual size-related borrowing cost advantages, while there appears to be no size-related borrowing cost advantage in non-trading financial industries.

The dramatic changes in the size effect documented in Table 10 suggest that liquidity-related factors explain an unusually large portion of the size effect during the crisis period. After controlling for liquidity, the size effect in banking *drops* in magnitude during the financial crisis to nearly zero. In contrast, the size effect in trading approximately doubles in size as compared to both the pre-crisis period and the sub-sample regressions from Table 6. The size effect for other financial industries does not respond significantly to liquidity-related controls.

## 5.2. Recovery rates

Our earlier analysis controls for default risk, but recovery rates - or their reverse, loss given default (LGD) - are another important component of credit risk. If larger firms have lower expected LGD, they should have lower CDS spreads holding default probabilities constant. LGD by itself is unlikely to fully explain the size effect; the important question is what causes changes in risk-neutral estimates of LGD. A firm could have a lower LGD due to the type of assets it has, due to public bailouts, or due to correlation between expected LGD and marginal utility. Determining whether LGD is related to borrower size cannot fully address these questions, but it can shed light on the avenue through which the size effect operates.

To consider these issues, we compare firm size to realized LGD. Our sample includes all default events from April 1987 to April 2013 from Moody's Analytics, Default and Recovery Database with LGD > 0. We classify firms into industries using the methodology outlined in Section 3. We calculate firm size as the face value of debt outstanding at the time of the default, which assumes that the value of equity is negligible during default. Table 11 documents the number of defaults by industry along with the average size and LGD.

As illustrated in Table 11, the three financial industries have few realized default observations. Additionally, these observations consist of relatively small firms (by contrast, Table 1 suggests financial firms in our CDS sample are relatively large). Because government intervention could occur to prevent failure, we are cautious about interpreting realized LGD results for financial institutions. However, the existence of a relationship between size and LGD[7] in other industries suggests the possibility that larger firms have higher recovery rates for non-bailout related reasons.

If large financial firms had a higher recovery rate than small financial firms even excluding the possibility of bailouts, then we would expect to see a size effect in financial industries. While we cannot empirically test this possibility due to the limited number of failures of large financial institutions, we can see that larger firms have higher recovery rates in other industries in situations that do not involve government intervention. If some of the same factors that apply to large non-financial firms also apply to large financial firms, then fundamental-based differences in recovery rates may drive part of the size effect. Future research is needed to identify the factors which drive the relationship between recovery rates and size and determine whether they would apply to the financial industry as well.

---

[7]In Appendix Table A.9, we present results of regressions of realized LGD on log size (Columns 1-3) and realized LGD on log size-industry interactions (Column 4). We find that larger firms have lower average LGD. Interacting size with industry variables suggests that this relationship holds for most industries, although it is statistically significant only for three: business equipment, consumer durables, and other non-financial.

# 6. Interpreting our results

Most of our analysis involves regressing log spread on log size interacted across industries. To help interpret the magnitude of our results, we consider the impact of a 10% increase in size on borrowing costs implied by our results. For coefficient $\beta$ on log of assets and a borrower with spread $s$, the change in spread implied by a 10% increase in assets is given by:

$$\frac{\Delta s}{s} = 1.1^\beta - 1. \tag{6}$$

In Table 12, we summarize results across these Tables 6, 8, and 10 in terms of the expected percentage change in borrowing costs from a 10% increase in assets. For the full sample, a 10% increase in size reduces borrowing costs for banking, trading, and other financial firms by approximately 1%, while this quantity is around 4% for firms in the shops, business equipment, and chemicals industries.

The effect for financial firms is highest (2.8%) for trading firms during the crisis when we control for liquidity (Table 10). This is the only case where our estimated size effect is highest in a financial industry. In other periods and other specifications, there is always a non-financial industry with a larger estimated size effect than that for the banking, trading, and other financial industries.

# 7. Conclusion

Our analysis examines both industry-specific and time-varying effects of borrower size on the cost of borrowing, using both CDS and corporate bond spreads over the period 2004 to 2013. Across industries, the largest borrowers enjoy borrowing cost advantages. Consideration of variation in the size effect across industries suggests that borrowing advantages for the largest financial firms do not seem unusual. With the exception of investment banking and trading firms during the recent financial crisis, the size effect is not generally largest for financial borrowers. We find qualitatively similar results using a variety of size measures including both continuous measures that adjust for firm size distribution with an industry and indicator variables identifying the largest borrowers. We present evidence that suggests the size effect is partially driven by liquidity and recovery rates.

Our results suggest that researchers may overestimate the size of too-big-to-fail subsidies if they do not take into account the lower borrowing costs of larger firms across a variety of industries. However, prior to the financial crisis, we also find that financial firms exhibited generally lower spreads that were less sensitive to size than spreads for several other industries. Our results suggest that estimates of implicit government guarantees to financial firms may overemphasize size-related borrowing cost differentials. This suggests that investor expectations of government support, or generally reduced risk perceptions, may have reduced borrowing costs for the financial industry, as a whole.

# References

Acharya, V., D. Anginer, and J. Warburton. 2013. The end of market discipline? Investor expectations of implicit state guarantees. *Working paper* .

Acharya, V. V., S. T. Bharath, and A. Srinivasan. 2007. Does industry-wide distress affect defaulted firms? Evidence from creditor recoveries. *Journal of Financial Economics* 85:787–821.

Araten, M., and C. Turner. 2013. Understanding the funding cost differences between global systemically important banks (GSIBs) and non-GSIBs in the USA. *Journal of Risk Management in Financial Institutions* pp. 387–410.

Banz, R. W. 1981. The relationship between return and market value of common stocks. *Journal of Financial Economics* 9:3–18.

Bassett, W. F. 2014. Using Insured Deposits to Refine Estimates of the Large Bank Funding Advantage. *Working paper* .

Berk, J. B. 1995. A critique of size-related anomalies. *Review of Financial Studies* 8:275–286.

Brewer III, E., and J. Jagtiani. 2013. How much did banks pay to become too-big-to-fail and to become systemically important? *Journal of Financial Services Research* 43:1–35.

Carey, M., and M. Gordy. 2009. The bank as grim reaper: Debt composition and bankruptcy thresholds. *Working paper* .

Chan, K., and N.-F. Chen. 1988. An Unconditional Asset-Pricing Test and the Role of Firm Size as an Instrumental Variable for Risk. *The Journal of Finance* 43:309–325.

Demirguc-Kunt, A., and H. Huizinga. 2013. Are banks too big to fail or too big to save? International evidence from equity prices and CDS spreads. *Journal of Banking and Finance* 37:875–894.

Dick-Nielsen, J., P. Feldhütter, and D. Lando. 2012. Corporate bond liquidity before and after the onset of the subprime crisis. *Journal of Financial Economics* 103:471–492.

Doshi, H. 2011. The term structure of recovery rates. *Working paper* .

Fama, E. F., and K. R. French. 1992. The cross-section of expected stock returns. *Journal of Finance* 47:427–462.

Flannery, M. J., and S. M. Sorescu. 1996. Evidence of bank market discipline in subordinated debenture yields: 1983–1991. *The Journal of Finance* 51:1347–1377.

Gandhi, P., and H. Lustig. forthcoming. Size anomalies in U.S. bank stock returns. *Journal of Finance* .

GAO, U. S. 2014. Evidence from the bond market on banks' "too-big-to-fail" subsidy. *GAO 14-621, United States Government Accountability Office Report to Congress* .

Gropp, R., H. Hakenes, and I. Schnabel. 2011. Competition, risk-shifting, and public bail-out policies. *Review of Financial Studies* 24:2084–2120.

Houweling, P., and T. Vorst. 2005. Pricing default swaps: Empirical evidence. *Journal of International Money and Finance* 24:1200–1225.

Hughes, J. P., and L. J. Mester. 2013. Who said large banks dont experience scale economies? Evidence from a risk-return-driven cost function. *Journal of Financial Intermediation* 22:559–585.

Hughes, J. P., L. J. Mester, and C.-G. Moon. 2001. Are scale economies in banking elusive or illusive?: Evidence obtained by incorporating capital structure and risk-taking into models of bank production. *Journal of Banking & Finance* 25:2169–2208.

Iyer, R., M. Puri, and N. Ryan. 2013. Do depositors monitor banks? *National Bureau of Economic Research Working Paper No. 19050* .

Jacewitz, S., and J. Pogach. 2012. Deposit rate advantages at the largest banks. *Working paper* .

Kelly, B. T., H. Lustig, and S. Van Nieuwerburgh. 2011. Too-systemic-to-fail: What option markets imply about sector-wide government guarantees. *National Bureau of Economic Research Working Paper No. 17149* .

Kovner, A., J. Vickery, and L. Zhou. 2014. Do big banks have lower operating costs? *Economic Policy Review* December.

Kroszner, R. S. 2013. A review of bank funding cost differentials. *Working paper* .

Li, Q. S., Zan, and J. Zhang. 2011. Quantifying the value of implicit government guarantees for large financial institutions. *Moody's Analytics Report* .

Merton, R. C. 1974. On the pricing of corporate debt: The risk structure of interest rates. *The Journal of Finance* 29:449–470.

Noss, J., and R. Sowerbutts. 2012. The implicit subsidy of banks. *Bank of England Financial Stability Paper* 15.

O'Hara, M., and W. Shaw. 1990. Deposit insurance and wealth effects: the value of being too big to fail. *The Journal of Finance* 45:1587–1600.

Penas, M., and H. Unal. 2004. Gains in bank mergers: Evidence from the bond markets. *Journal of Financial Economics* 74:149–179.

Santos, J. 2014. Evidence from the bond market on banks' "too-big-to-fail" subsidy. *Economic Policy Review* 20.

Tsesmelidakis, Z., and R. C. Merton. 2013. The value of implicit guarantees. *Working Paper*

.


Ueda, K., and B. Weder di Mauro. 2013. Quantifying structural subsidy values for systemi-

cally important financial institutions. *Journal of Banking & Finance* 37:3830–3842.

Wheelock, D. C., and P. W. Wilson. 2012. Do large banks have lower costs? New estimates

of returns to scale for US banks. *Journal of Money, Credit and Banking* 44:171–199.

Table 1: **CDS sample means**

| Industry | Spread | EDF | LogSize | StdSize | Leverage | Depth | Raise | Size95 | Rating |
|---|---|---|---|---|---|---|---|---|---|
| Banking | 178 | 1.53 | 12.1 | 2.1 | 63.6 | 5.9 | 30.0 | 0.5 | 22.3 |
| Other Financial | 269 | 1.58 | 10.6 | 1.2 | 28.9 | 7.2 | 2.6 | 0.2 | 21.5 |
| Trading | 206 | 1.18 | 9.2 | 1.1 | 47.5 | 5.1 | 3.3 | 0.2 | 19.5 |
| Business Equipment | 167 | 0.70 | 9.4 | 1.8 | 18.5 | 5.5 | 4.1 | 0.7 | 19.4 |
| Chemicals | 128 | 0.70 | 9.0 | 1.7 | 20.2 | 6.4 | 5.1 | 0.4 | 21.1 |
| Consumer Durables | 401 | 2.38 | 8.7 | 1.0 | 37.0 | 5.7 | 0.8 | 0.1 | 19.4 |
| Consumer Non-Durables | 202 | 1.04 | 8.8 | 1.2 | 27.8 | 6.5 | 1.8 | 0.2 | 19.7 |
| Energy | 152 | 1.00 | 9.5 | 1.4 | 24.3 | 6.6 | 2.5 | 0.3 | 18.7 |
| Health Care | 164 | 0.50 | 8.8 | 1.7 | 25.9 | 5.8 | 2.4 | 0.6 | 17.6 |
| Manufacturing | 165 | 0.91 | 8.9 | 1.2 | 26.2 | 6.1 | 1.4 | 0.2 | 20.8 |
| Other Non-Financial | 347 | 2.38 | 9.0 | 1.5 | 36.9 | 6.2 | 1.9 | 0.5 | 18.1 |
| Shops | 222 | 1.14 | 9.0 | 1.3 | 27.1 | 7.2 | 2.0 | 0.4 | 18.0 |
| Telecommunications | 302 | 2.04 | 9.5 | 0.9 | 46.5 | 6.0 | 3.9 | 0.2 | 17.1 |
| Utilities | 119 | 0.55 | 9.7 | 0.8 | 46.5 | 5.8 | 1.6 | 0.1 | 20.1 |

The underlying CDS sample consists of 17,486 quarter-firm observations and 665 firms. Variables include 5-year CDS spread, expected default probability (EDF), log assets, standardized log assets (measures size in units of standard deviation from the mean of log of assets for Compustat firms in the same industry), market leverage, CDS depth (a measure of the amount of trading in comparable CDS contracts), sum of debt raised over past 5 years (Raise, $M), an indicator for 95th percentile of size across within-industry Compustat firms, and credit rating (expressed on a 1-28 scale with 28=AAA). See Appendix Table A.1. for more detailed variable definitions. Non-financial firms are classified according to the Fama-French 12 industry classifications. Financial firms (which fall under the "Money" Fama-French 12 industry classification) are further classified into banking, trading, and other financial based on the Fama-French 48 industry classifications.

Table 2: **Bond sample means**

| Industry | Spread | EDF | LogSize | StdSize | Leverage | Maturity | Size95 | Rating |
|---|---|---|---|---|---|---|---|---|
| Banking | 218 | 1.2 | 13.1 | 2.6 | 70.1 | 6.6 | 0.70 | 22.3 |
| Other Financial | 291 | 1.1 | 10.5 | 1.1 | 29.7 | 9.8 | 0.11 | 19.6 |
| Trading | 166 | 0.8 | 13.0 | 2.4 | 85.5 | 4.2 | 0.79 | 22.6 |
| Business Equipment | 167 | 0.8 | 10.2 | 2.1 | 16.0 | 8.8 | 0.85 | 21.0 |
| Chemicals | 142 | 0.5 | 10.5 | 2.3 | 19.5 | 9.2 | 0.82 | 23.0 |
| Consumer Durables | 628 | 1.4 | 12.0 | 2.0 | 71.5 | 21.2 | 0.89 | 13.5 |
| Consumer Non-Durables | 190 | 0.2 | 9.7 | 1.5 | 24.0 | 9.8 | 0.56 | 20.2 |
| Energy | 227 | 0.6 | 9.9 | 1.6 | 20.7 | 20.0 | 0.73 | 19.5 |
| Health Care | 203 | 0.2 | 8.8 | 1.7 | 14.0 | 10.3 | 0.81 | 20.5 |
| Manufacturing | 202 | 0.8 | 9.9 | 1.6 | 28.4 | 10.5 | 0.65 | 19.8 |
| Other Non-Financial | 334 | 2.3 | 9.8 | 1.8 | 37.9 | 7.3 | 0.74 | 17.7 |
| Shops | 190 | 0.6 | 10.6 | 2.0 | 24.6 | 9.4 | 0.72 | 21.0 |
| Telecommunications | 425 | 10.4 | 9.1 | 1.0 | 44.7 | 3.6 | 0.04 | 15.8 |
| Utilities | 253 | 0.6 | 9.4 | 0.7 | 50.1 | 7.9 | 0.05 | 17.2 |

The underlying bond sample consists of 16,006 quarter-firm observations and 319 firms. Variables include bond spread, expected default probability (EDF), log assets, standardized log assets (measures size in units of standard deviation from the mean of log of assets for Compustat firms in the same industry), market leverage, bond maturity in years, an indicator for 95th percentile of size across within-industry Compustat firms, and credit rating (expressed on a 1-28 scale with 28=AAA). See Appendix Table A.1. for more detailed variable definitions. Non-financial firms are classified according to the Fama-French 12 Industry classifications. Financial firms (which fall under the "Money" Fama-French 12 industry classification) are further classified into banking, trading, and other financial based on the Fama-French 48 industry classifications.

Table 3: **Number of unique firms by industry and year**

| Industry | 2004 | 2005 | 2006 | 2007 | 2008 | 2009 | 2010 | 2011 | 2012 | 2013 |
|---|---|---|---|---|---|---|---|---|---|---|
| Panel A: CDS sample | | | | | | | | | | |
| Banking | 12 | 15 | 18 | 20 | 20 | 18 | 18 | 18 | 19 | 19 |
| Other Financial | 28 | 31 | 37 | 39 | 39 | 35 | 34 | 34 | 32 | 31 |
| Trading | 23 | 27 | 32 | 39 | 39 | 35 | 35 | 36 | 37 | 32 |
| Business Equipment | 30 | 36 | 46 | 49 | 43 | 38 | 35 | 34 | 33 | 34 |
| Chemicals | 36 | 45 | 49 | 52 | 50 | 44 | 39 | 35 | 36 | 35 |
| Consumer Durables | 10 | 11 | 14 | 14 | 15 | 14 | 13 | 13 | 12 | 9 |
| Consumer Non-Durables | 29 | 32 | 36 | 37 | 36 | 33 | 32 | 33 | 33 | 33 |
| Energy | 23 | 25 | 27 | 33 | 33 | 31 | 30 | 28 | 28 | 23 |
| Health Care | 11 | 11 | 14 | 16 | 16 | 14 | 13 | 13 | 14 | 12 |
| Manufacturing | 58 | 61 | 69 | 75 | 72 | 67 | 66 | 63 | 60 | 56 |
| Other Non-Financial | 46 | 53 | 64 | 69 | 71 | 67 | 67 | 62 | 65 | 59 |
| Shops | 42 | 44 | 50 | 54 | 52 | 45 | 45 | 41 | 41 | 40 |
| Telecommunications | 15 | 18 | 24 | 29 | 30 | 25 | 22 | 17 | 17 | 17 |
| Utilities | 33 | 36 | 41 | 45 | 45 | 46 | 48 | 43 | 40 | 35 |
| Panel B: Bond sample | | | | | | | | | | |
| Banking | 22 | 25 | 34 | 32 | 30 | 27 | 25 | 31 | 29 | 25 |
| Other Financial | 16 | 21 | 28 | 28 | 24 | 21 | 19 | 17 | 15 | 13 |
| Trading | 7 | 10 | 12 | 10 | 12 | 6 | 6 | 6 | 5 | 3 |
| Business Equipment | 10 | 12 | 15 | 13 | 8 | 8 | 6 | 4 | 4 | 4 |
| Chemicals | 12 | 17 | 22 | 22 | 17 | 12 | 10 | 9 | 9 | 6 |
| Consumer Durables | 2 | 2 | 4 | 3 | 3 | 2 | 3 | 3 | 2 | 2 |
| Consumer Non-Durables | 15 | 17 | 21 | 15 | 15 | 15 | 13 | 12 | 12 | 12 |
| Energy | 5 | 3 | 8 | 7 | 6 | 6 | 4 | 5 | 4 | 4 |
| Health Care | 3 | 4 | 5 | 4 | 4 | 3 | 3 | 3 | 3 | 3 |
| Manufacturing | 16 | 23 | 26 | 23 | 22 | 23 | 22 | 21 | 17 | 11 |
| Other Non-Financial | 16 | 21 | 26 | 22 | 20 | 14 | 14 | 13 | 13 | 10 |
| Shops | 17 | 21 | 23 | 20 | 13 | 12 | 11 | 12 | 8 | 8 |
| Telecommunications | 4 | 7 | 7 | 6 | 3 | 2 | 2 | 1 | 2 | 1 |
| Utilities | 4 | 8 | 20 | 16 | 8 | 6 | 7 | 4 | 3 | 1 |

Table 4: **Regressions of log CDS spread on firm size for banking and trading financial firms**

|  | (1) Full | (2) Full | (3) Full | (4) Pre-Crisis | (5) Crisis | (6) Post-Crisis |
|---|---|---|---|---|---|---|
| EDF | 0.042 (***) | 0.072 (***) | 0.073 (***) | 0.088 (***) | 0.081 (***) | 0.063 (***) |
|  | (0.003) | (0.005) | (0.005) | (0.009) | (0.008) | (0.005) |
| Banking | 0.045 | 0.057 | 0.116 | -0.158 (***) | 0.985 (**) | 0.147 |
|  | (0.126) | (0.088) | (0.110) | (0.055) | (0.460) | (0.175) |
| Banking*EDF |  |  | -0.022 (*) | 0.031 | -0.032 | -0.040 (**) |
|  |  |  | (0.012) | (0.035) | (0.022) | (0.016) |
| Banking*EDF$^2$ |  |  | 0.000 | -0.006 | 0.001 | 0.001 |
|  |  |  | (0.001) | (0.004) | (0.001) | (0.001) |
| EDF$^2$ |  | -0.001 (***) | -0.001 (***) | -0.002 (***) | -0.001 (***) | -0.001 (**) |
|  |  | (0.000) | (0.000) | (0.001) | (0.000) | (0.000) |
| LogSize | -0.016 (***) | -0.012 (***) | -0.011 (***) | -0.014 (***) | 0.026 (***) | -0.018 (***) |
|  | (0.004) | (0.004) | (0.004) | (0.004) | (0.009) | (0.004) |
| LogSize*Banking | -0.005 | -0.006 | -0.009 | 0.011 (**) | -0.083 (**) | -0.006 |
|  | (0.010) | (0.007) | (0.009) | (0.005) | (0.036) | (0.014) |
| LogSize*Trading | 0.002 | -0.005 | -0.005 | 0.002 | -0.062 (***) | 0.001 |
|  | (0.006) | (0.006) | (0.006) | (0.005) | (0.017) | (0.007) |
| Trading | -0.033 | 0.029 | 0.039 | -0.059 | 0.658 (***) | -0.004 |
|  | (0.051) | (0.052) | (0.052) | (0.047) | (0.157) | (0.069) |
| Trading*EDF |  |  | -0.005 | 0.081 (*) | -0.004 | -0.015 (*) |
|  |  |  | (0.009) | (0.044) | (0.019) | (0.007) |
| Trading*EDF$^2$ |  |  | 0.000 | -0.014 (**) | -0.000 | 0.000 |
|  |  |  | (0.000) | (0.006) | (0.001) | (0.000) |
| Adj.R$^2$ | 0.585 | 0.618 | 0.621 | 0.571 | 0.625 | 0.628 |
| N | 17,486 | 17,486 | 17,486 | 8,227 | 1,984 | 7,275 |

This table presents results from estimating Equation 1 for CDS sample over the full time sample (04Q1-13Q2, Columns 1-3) and for the pre-crisis sample (04Q1-08Q2, Column 4), the financial crisis sample (08Q3-09Q2, Column 5), and the post-crisis sample (09Q3-13Q2, Column 6). EDF is the expected default frequency, Log-Size is log of book assets, and Banking and Trading represent industry indicator variables. All specifications include industry and quarter fixed effects and report standard errors clustered at the firm level. ***, **, and * indicate statistical significance at the 1%, 5% and 10% levels, respectively.

Table 5: **Regressions of log bond spread on firm size for banking and trading financial firms**

| | (1) Full | (2) Full | (3) Full | (4) Pre-Crisis | (5) Crisis | (6) Post-Crisis |
|---|---|---|---|---|---|---|
| EDF | 0.022 (***) | 0.055 (***) | 0.069 (***) | 0.062 (***) | 0.090 (***) | 0.078 (***) |
| | (0.002) | (0.008) | (0.005) | (0.008) | (0.009) | (0.010) |
| Banking | -0.212 (**) | -0.148 (*) | -0.091 | -0.086 | 0.165 | -0.287 (**) |
| | (0.096) | (0.083) | (0.081) | (0.061) | (0.247) | (0.130) |
| Banking*EDF | | | -0.026 (**) | 0.052 (**) | -0.060 (***) | -0.012 |
| | | | (0.012) | (0.021) | (0.015) | (0.013) |
| Banking*EDF$^2$ | | | 0.001 (*) | -0.005 (***) | 0.002 (***) | 0.001 (**) |
| | | | (0.000) | (0.002) | (0.001) | (0.001) |
| EDF$^2$ | | -0.001 (***) | -0.002 (***) | -0.001 (***) | -0.002 (***) | -0.003 (***) |
| | | (0.000) | (0.000) | (0.000) | (0.000) | (0.001) |
| LogSize | -0.044 (***) | -0.036 (***) | -0.033 (***) | -0.018 (***) | -0.052 (***) | -0.048 (***) |
| | (0.005) | (0.005) | (0.005) | (0.005) | (0.008) | (0.006) |
| LogSize*Banking | 0.023 (***) | 0.015 (**) | 0.011 (*) | 0.006 | -0.001 | 0.029 (***) |
| | (0.008) | (0.007) | (0.007) | (0.006) | (0.019) | (0.010) |
| LogSize*Trading | 0.036 (***) | 0.029 (***) | 0.026 (***) | 0.014 (**) | 0.025 | 0.040 (***) |
| | (0.009) | (0.009) | (0.009) | (0.006) | (0.026) | (0.012) |
| Maturity | 0.001 (***) | 0.001 (***) | 0.001 (***) | 0.001 (***) | -0.001 (**) | 0.001 (***) |
| | (0.000) | (0.000) | (0.000) | (0.000) | (0.001) | (0.000) |
| Trading | -0.398 (***) | -0.332 (***) | -0.268 (**) | -0.172 (***) | -0.137 | -0.450 (***) |
| | (0.113) | (0.116) | (0.113) | (0.064) | (0.340) | (0.162) |
| Trading*EDF | | | -0.044 (***) | -0.011 | -0.071 (***) | 0.024 |
| | | | (0.014) | (0.013) | (0.015) | (0.041) |
| Trading*EDF$^2$ | | | 0.001 (**) | -0.003 (***) | 0.002 (***) | -0.014 |
| | | | (0.000) | (0.001) | (0.001) | (0.010) |
| Adj.R$^2$ | 0.610 | 0.648 | 0.659 | 0.610 | 0.573 | 0.657 |
| N | 15,972 | 15,972 | 15,972 | 8,303 | 1,831 | 5,838 |

This table presents results from estimating Equation 2 for bond trading (TRACE) sample over the full sample (04Q1-13Q2, Columns 1-3) and for pre-crisis (04Q1-08Q2, Column 4), financial crisis (08Q3-09Q2, Column 5), and post-crisis (09Q3-13Q2, Column 6) subsamples. EDF is the expected default frequency, LogSize is log of book assets, and Banking and Trading represent industry indicator variables. All specifications include industry and quarter fixed effects and report standard errors clustered at the firm level. ***, **, and * indicate statistical significance at the 1%, 5% and 10% levels, respectively.

Table 6: **Regression of log CDS spread on firm size across industries and time periods**

|  | (1) Full | (2) Pre-Crisis | (3) Crisis | (4) Post-Crisis |
|---|---|---|---|---|
| LogSize* Banking | -0.020 (**) | -0.003 | -0.057 (*) | -0.024 (*) |
|  | (0.008) | (0.003) | (0.035) | (0.013) |
| LogSize* Other Financial | -0.014 (*) | -0.009 (***) | 0.037 (**) | -0.036 (***) |
|  | (0.007) | (0.003) | (0.015) | (0.013) |
| LogSize* Trading | -0.016 (***) | -0.013 (***) | -0.036 (***) | -0.017 (***) |
|  | (0.004) | (0.003) | (0.014) | (0.006) |
| LogSize* Business Equipment | -0.030 (***) | -0.032 (***) | -0.000 | -0.028 (***) |
|  | (0.006) | (0.007) | (0.012) | (0.008) |
| LogSize* Chemicals | -0.027 (***) | -0.030 (***) | -0.012 | -0.021 (***) |
|  | (0.007) | (0.006) | (0.011) | (0.006) |
| LogSize* Consumer Durables | 0.066 (***) | 0.059 (***) | 0.199 (***) | 0.024 (*) |
|  | (0.017) | (0.015) | (0.063) | (0.014) |
| LogSize* Consumer Non-Durables | -0.034 (**) | -0.009 | 0.003 | -0.042 (***) |
|  | (0.014) | (0.010) | (0.032) | (0.013) |
| LogSize* Energy | -0.023 (***) | -0.022 (***) | -0.013 | -0.029 (**) |
|  | (0.007) | (0.006) | (0.014) | (0.012) |
| LogSize* Health Care | -0.024 | -0.004 | -0.028 | -0.052 (**) |
|  | (0.018) | (0.009) | (0.029) | (0.022) |
| LogSize* Manufacturing | -0.012 (**) | -0.013 (***) | 0.004 | -0.016 (***) |
|  | (0.005) | (0.005) | (0.015) | (0.006) |
| LogSize* Other Non-Financial | 0.003 | 0.003 | 0.036 (***) | -0.008 |
|  | (0.007) | (0.010) | (0.013) | (0.007) |
| LogSize* Shops | -0.044 (***) | -0.045 (***) | -0.001 | -0.030 (**) |
|  | (0.014) | (0.017) | (0.017) | (0.014) |
| LogSize* Telecommunications | -0.011 | -0.004 | -0.003 | -0.029 (*) |
|  | (0.011) | (0.013) | (0.014) | (0.015) |
| LogSize* Utilities | 0.004 | 0.000 | 0.016 | 0.004 |
|  | (0.006) | (0.006) | (0.016) | (0.009) |
| Adj.$R^2$ | 0.665 | 0.646 | 0.675 | 0.719 |
| N | 17,486 | 8,227 | 1,984 | 7,275 |

This table presents results of estimating Equation 3 across the financial crisis (2008Q3-2009Q2), pre-crisis (2004Q1-2008Q2), and post-crisis (2009Q3-2013Q2) subsamples. Specifications include industry and quarter fixed effects and interactions between industry and EDF and industry and $EDF^2$. Standard errors are clustered at the firm level. ***, **, and * indicate statistical significance at the 1%, 5% and 10% levels, respectively.

Table 7: **Regression of log CDS spread across industries and time period, nonlinear size effect**

|  | (1) Full | (2) Pre-Crisis | (3) Crisis | (4) Post-Crisis |
|---|---|---|---|---|
| LogSize* Banking | -0.012 | 0.001 | -0.032 | -0.016 |
|  | (0.011) | (0.004) | (0.044) | (0.018) |
| Size95* Banking | -0.035 | -0.017 | -0.115 | -0.033 |
|  | (0.023) | (0.012) | (0.099) | (0.036) |
| LogSize* Other Financial | -0.012 | -0.006 | 0.013 | -0.031 (**) |
|  | (0.011) | (0.005) | (0.033) | (0.015) |
| Size95* Other Financial | -0.010 | -0.015 | 0.119 | -0.028 |
|  | (0.029) | (0.013) | (0.112) | (0.046) |
| LogSize* Trading | -0.014 (**) | -0.010 | -0.031 | -0.013 |
|  | (0.007) | (0.007) | (0.022) | (0.009) |
| Size95* Trading | -0.010 | -0.012 | -0.026 | -0.019 |
|  | (0.030) | (0.033) | (0.114) | (0.030) |
| LogSize* Business Equipment | -0.029 (***) | -0.031 (***) | -0.020 | -0.025 (***) |
|  | (0.006) | (0.008) | (0.021) | (0.007) |
| Size95* Business Equipment | -0.002 | -0.004 | 0.064 | -0.013 |
|  | (0.027) | (0.027) | (0.089) | (0.026) |
| LogSize* Chemicals | -0.026 (**) | -0.029 (***) | -0.014 | -0.018 (*) |
|  | (0.011) | (0.010) | (0.021) | (0.011) |
| Size95* Chemicals | -0.003 | -0.003 | 0.005 | -0.009 |
|  | (0.018) | (0.019) | (0.042) | (0.024) |
| LogSize* Consumer Durables | 0.015 | 0.002 | 0.044 | -0.020 |
|  | (0.026) | (0.024) | (0.070) | (0.016) |
| Size95* Consumer Durables | 0.288 (***) | 0.308 (***) | 0.988 (***) | 0.240 (***) |
|  | (0.109) | (0.097) | (0.277) | (0.070) |
| LogSize* Consumer Non-Durables | -0.033 | -0.009 | 0.047 | -0.040 (*) |
|  | (0.021) | (0.015) | (0.052) | (0.021) |
| Size95* Consumer Non-Durables | -0.005 | -0.000 | -0.167 (*) | -0.007 |
|  | (0.038) | (0.026) | (0.093) | (0.040) |
| LogSize* Energy | -0.028 (***) | -0.028 (***) | -0.018 | -0.043 (***) |
|  | (0.007) | (0.008) | (0.017) | (0.012) |
| Size95* Energy | 0.018 | 0.019 | 0.016 | 0.041 |
|  | (0.019) | (0.014) | (0.050) | (0.028) |
| LogSize* Health Care | -0.022 | 0.013 | -0.054 | -0.067 (***) |
|  | (0.016) | (0.010) | (0.036) | (0.026) |
| Size95* Health Care | -0.004 | -0.037 (**) | 0.059 | 0.030 |
|  | (0.019) | (0.015) | (0.051) | (0.023) |
| LogSize* Manufacturing | -0.002 | -0.003 | 0.033 | -0.010 |
|  | (0.010) | (0.010) | (0.028) | (0.009) |
| Size95* Manufacturing | -0.033 (*) | -0.028 | -0.093 | -0.023 |
|  | (0.019) | (0.020) | (0.061) | (0.020) |

Table 7: **Regression of log CDS spread across industries and time period, nonlinear size effect**

|  | (1) Full | (2) Pre-Crisis | (3) Crisis | (4) Post-Crisis |
|---|---|---|---|---|
| LogSize* Other Non-Financial | 0.008 | 0.011 | 0.038 (**) | 0.001 |
|  | (0.010) | (0.016) | (0.019) | (0.008) |
| Size95* Other Non-Financial | -0.019 | -0.024 | -0.008 | -0.028 |
|  | (0.024) | (0.031) | (0.061) | (0.023) |
| LogSize* Shops | -0.056 (***) | -0.056 (**) | 0.008 | -0.039 (**) |
|  | (0.021) | (0.027) | (0.032) | (0.017) |
| Size95* Shops | 0.034 | 0.028 | -0.022 | 0.025 |
|  | (0.028) | (0.032) | (0.050) | (0.036) |
| LogSize* Telecommunications | 0.018 | 0.041 | 0.035 | -0.016 |
|  | (0.020) | (0.027) | (0.026) | (0.023) |
| Size95* Telecommunications | -0.140 (**) | -0.214 (**) | -0.182 (**) | -0.056 |
|  | (0.062) | (0.091) | (0.081) | (0.054) |
| LogSize* Utilities | 0.009 | 0.003 | 0.024 | 0.010 |
|  | (0.008) | (0.007) | (0.018) | (0.012) |
| Size95* Utilities | -0.023 | -0.016 | -0.054 | -0.022 |
|  | (0.018) | (0.013) | (0.048) | (0.022) |
| Adj.$R^2$ | 0.668 | 0.653 | 0.684 | 0.721 |
| N | 17,486 | 8,227 | 1,984 | 7,275 |

This table presents results of estimating Equation 4 over crisis (2008Q3-2009Q2), pre-crisis (2004Q1-2008Q2), and post-crisis (2009Q3-2013Q2) subsamples. Regression specifications augment Equation 3 with an additional size variable (Size95) to examine nonlinear size effects for the largest firms in each industry. Specifications include industry and quarter fixed effects and interactions between industry and EDF and industry and $EDF^2$. Standard errors are clustered at the firm level. ***, **, and * indicate statistical significance at the 1%, 5% and 10% levels, respectively.

Table 8: **Regression of log bond spread on firm size across industries and time periods**

| | (1) Full | (2) Pre-Crisis | (3) Crisis | (4) Post-Crisis |
|---|---|---|---|---|
| LogSize* Banking | -0.021 (***) | -0.011 (***) | -0.052 (***) | -0.019 (**) |
| | (0.005) | (0.003) | (0.016) | (0.008) |
| LogSize* Other Financial | -0.034 (***) | -0.018 (***) | -0.030 | -0.068 (***) |
| | (0.011) | (0.007) | (0.021) | (0.021) |
| LogSize* Trading | -0.007 | -0.004 | -0.027 | -0.007 |
| | (0.008) | (0.003) | (0.025) | (0.011) |
| LogSize* Business Equipment | -0.013 | 0.017 | 0.013 | -0.073 (***) |
| | (0.021) | (0.024) | (0.041) | (0.006) |
| LogSize* Chemicals | -0.020 (**) | -0.013 | -0.036 (**) | -0.031 |
| | (0.010) | (0.009) | (0.015) | (0.020) |
| LogSize* Consumer Durables | 0.005 | -0.026 | 0.036 | 0.007 |
| | (0.033) | (0.035) | (0.046) | (0.028) |
| LogSize* Consumer Non-Durables | -0.025 | -0.015 | -0.016 | -0.032 |
| | (0.016) | (0.012) | (0.034) | (0.020) |
| LogSize* Energy | -0.002 | -0.005 | 0.071 (**) | 0.018 |
| | (0.013) | (0.008) | (0.032) | (0.023) |
| LogSize* Health Care | -0.015 | -0.006 | -0.045 | -0.018 (***) |
| | (0.023) | (0.004) | (0.029) | (0.006) |
| LogSize* Manufacturing | -0.050 (***) | -0.030 (***) | -0.051 (***) | -0.052 (***) |
| | (0.011) | (0.009) | (0.019) | (0.013) |
| LogSize* Other Non-Financial | -0.039 (***) | -0.029 (***) | -0.071 (***) | -0.044 (***) |
| | (0.006) | (0.007) | (0.013) | (0.007) |
| LogSize* Shops | -0.048 (***) | -0.017 (*) | -0.064 (***) | -0.059 (***) |
| | (0.008) | (0.009) | (0.014) | (0.011) |
| LogSize* Telecommunications | -0.016 (**) | -0.020 (**) | -0.046 (***) | -0.028 (***) |
| | (0.007) | (0.010) | (0.014) | (0.002) |
| LogSize* Utilities | 0.009 | 0.004 | -0.009 | 0.029 |
| | (0.009) | (0.007) | (0.022) | (0.033) |
| Maturity | 0.001 (***) | 0.001 (***) | -0.001 (**) | 0.001 (***) |
| | (0.000) | (0.000) | (0.001) | (0.000) |
| Adj.$R^2$ | 0.677 | 0.643 | 0.608 | 0.679 |
| N | 15,972 | 8,303 | 1,831 | 5,838 |

This table presents results of regressions of (log) yield spread using bond trading data from TRACE on firm size (Equation 3). Pre-crisis period is 2004Q1-2008Q2, financial crisis period is 2008Q3-2009Q2, post-crisis period is 2009Q3-2013Q2. All specifications control for maturity and include industry interactions for EDF and $EDF^2$ as well as industry and year-quarter fixed effects. Standard errors are clustered at the firm level. ***, **, and * indicate statistical significance at the 1%, 5% and 10% levels, respectively.

Table 9: **Regression of log bond spread across industries and time period, nonlinear size effect**

| | (1) Full | (2) Pre-Crisis | (3) Crisis | (4) Post-Crisis |
|---|---|---|---|---|
| LogSize* Banking | -0.010 (*) | -0.005 | -0.020 | -0.020 (*) |
| | (0.005) | (0.003) | (0.019) | (0.011) |
| Size95* Banking | -0.042 (**) | -0.025 (**) | -0.130 (*) | 0.006 |
| | (0.020) | (0.011) | (0.072) | (0.032) |
| LogSize* Other Financial | -0.029 (**) | -0.007 | -0.018 | -0.059 (***) |
| | (0.015) | (0.009) | (0.028) | (0.020) |
| Size95* Other Financial | -0.023 | -0.040 | -0.066 | -0.132 (**) |
| | (0.033) | (0.028) | (0.058) | (0.057) |
| LogSize* Trading | -0.008 | -0.004 | -0.029 | -0.114 (***) |
| | (0.008) | (0.003) | (0.026) | (0.030) |
| Size95* Trading | 0.009 | 0.003 | 0.013 | 0.528 (***) |
| | (0.006) | (0.003) | (0.039) | (0.146) |
| LogSize* Business Equipment | -0.023 | 0.025 | -0.011 | -0.077 (***) |
| | (0.020) | (0.031) | (0.041) | (0.005) |
| Size95* Business Equipment | 0.071 | -0.037 | 0.155 | 0.579 (**) |
| | (0.096) | (0.083) | (0.165) | (0.231) |
| LogSize* Chemicals | -0.020 | -0.009 | -0.058 (**) | -0.051 (*) |
| | (0.013) | (0.009) | (0.026) | (0.030) |
| Size95* Chemicals | 0.002 | -0.018 | 0.090 | 0.085 |
| | (0.045) | (0.034) | (0.080) | (0.084) |
| LogSize* Consumer Durables | -0.126 (***) | -0.172 (***) | -0.257 (***) | -0.082 (***) |
| | (0.034) | (0.017) | (0.038) | (0.004) |
| Size95* Consumer Durables | 0.598 (***) | 0.733 (***) | 1.121 (***) | 0.427 (***) |
| | (0.098) | (0.080) | (0.133) | (0.020) |
| LogSize* Consumer Non-Durables | 0.001 | 0.006 | -0.001 | 0.002 |
| | (0.014) | (0.012) | (0.046) | (0.029) |
| Size95* Consumer Non-Durables | -0.060 (*) | -0.057 (*) | -0.033 | -0.072 |
| | (0.033) | (0.032) | (0.113) | (0.057) |
| LogSize* Energy | -0.016 | -0.012 | 0.115 (**) | -0.006 |
| | (0.012) | (0.008) | (0.055) | (0.031) |
| Size95* Energy | 0.068 (***) | 0.025 (*) | -0.059 | 0.055 (*) |
| | (0.015) | (0.013) | (0.043) | (0.033) |
| LogSize* Health Care | -0.047 | -0.001 | -2.372 (***) | 0.016 |
| | (0.031) | (0.009) | (0.786) | (0.014) |
| Size95* Health Care | 0.056 | -0.010 | 2.545 (***) | -0.044 (**) |
| | (0.035) | (0.016) | (0.838) | (0.019) |
| LogSize* Manufacturing | -0.033 (***) | 0.005 | -0.032 | -0.045 (***) |
| | (0.011) | (0.013) | (0.027) | (0.016) |
| Size95* Manufacturing | -0.044 (*) | -0.078 (***) | -0.045 | -0.018 |
| | (0.027) | (0.025) | (0.063) | (0.036) |

Table 9: **Regression of log bond spread across industries and time period, nonlinear size effect**

|  | (1) Full | (2) Pre-Crisis | (3) Crisis | (4) Post-Crisis |
|---|---|---|---|---|
| LogSize* Other Non-Financial | -0.035 (***) | -0.029 (***) | -0.058 (***) | -0.043 (***) |
|  | (0.005) | (0.007) | (0.013) | (0.006) |
| Size95* Other Non-Financial | -0.023 | 0.003 | -0.064 | -0.013 |
|  | (0.020) | (0.013) | (0.061) | (0.030) |
| LogSize* Shops | -0.043 (***) | -0.018 (*) | -0.071 (***) | -0.035 (***) |
|  | (0.009) | (0.010) | (0.010) | (0.009) |
| Size95* Shops | -0.019 | 0.003 | 0.038 | -0.097 (***) |
|  | (0.024) | (0.021) | (0.059) | (0.027) |
| LogSize* Telecommunications | -0.014 (**) | -0.019 (**) | -0.045 (***) | -0.028 (***) |
|  | (0.007) | (0.009) | (0.013) | (0.002) |
| Size95* Telecommunications | -0.057 (**) | -0.028 (*) | 0.000 | 0.000 |
|  | (0.024) | (0.016) | (0.000) | (0.000) |
| LogSize* Utilities | 0.013 | 0.008 | -0.009 | 0.029 |
|  | (0.009) | (0.008) | (0.022) | (0.033) |
| Size95* Utilities | -0.051 (***) | -0.041 (**) | 0.000 | 0.000 |
|  | (0.016) | (0.020) | (0.000) | (0.000) |
| Maturity | 0.001 (***) | 0.001 (***) | -0.001 (**) | 0.001 (***) |
|  | (0.000) | (0.000) | (0.001) | (0.000) |
| Adj.$R^2$ | 0.684 | 0.652 | 0.620 | 0.690 |
| N | 15,972 | 8,303 | 1,831 | 5,838 |

This table presents results of estimating Equation 4 using bond trading data from TRACE over financial crisis (2008Q3-2009Q2), pre-crisis (2004Q1-2008Q2) and post-crisis (2009Q3-2013Q2) subsamples. Regression specifications augment Equation 3 with an additional size variable (Size95) to examine nonlinear size effects for the largest firms in each industry. All specifications control for maturity and include industry interactions for EDF and $EDF^2$ as well as industry and year-quarter fixed effects. Standard errors are clustered at the firm level. ***, **, and * indicate statistical significance at the 1%, 5% and 10% levels, respectively.

Fig. 1. CDS pre-crisis size-industry coefficients

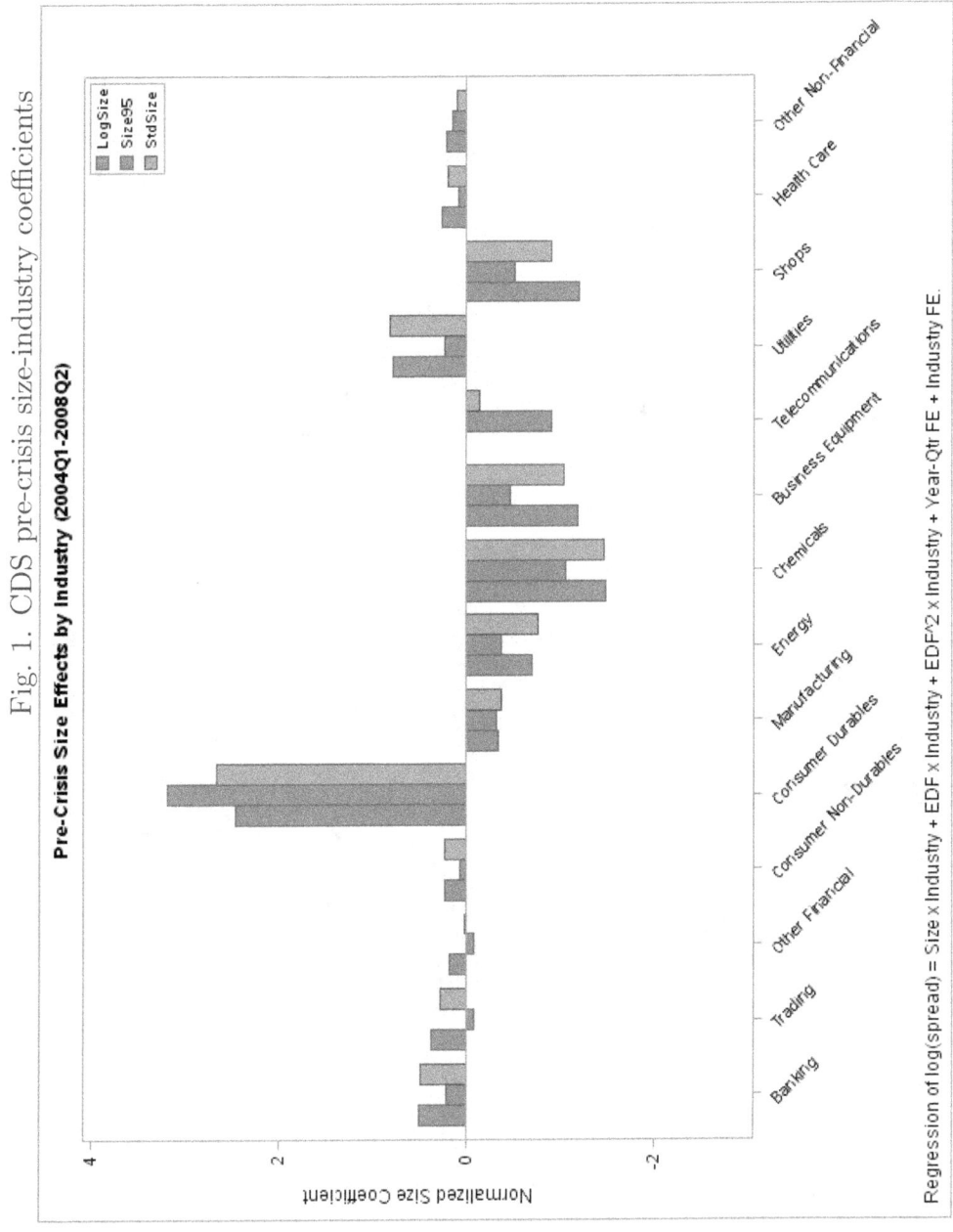

This figure presents coefficients on the size-industry interactions for the CDS pre-crisis subsample for three size variables - log size from Equation 3 (shown in blue), the Size95 indicator from Equation 4 (shown in red), and a standardized size variable (shown in green) which measures the number of standard deviations a firm's size is from the mean log assets of its industry. For ease of comparison, the coefficients are normalized by subtracting the mean value of the coefficients for a given size variable and dividing by the standard deviation of the coefficients. This figure presents coefficients

Fig. 2. CDS crisis size-industry coefficients

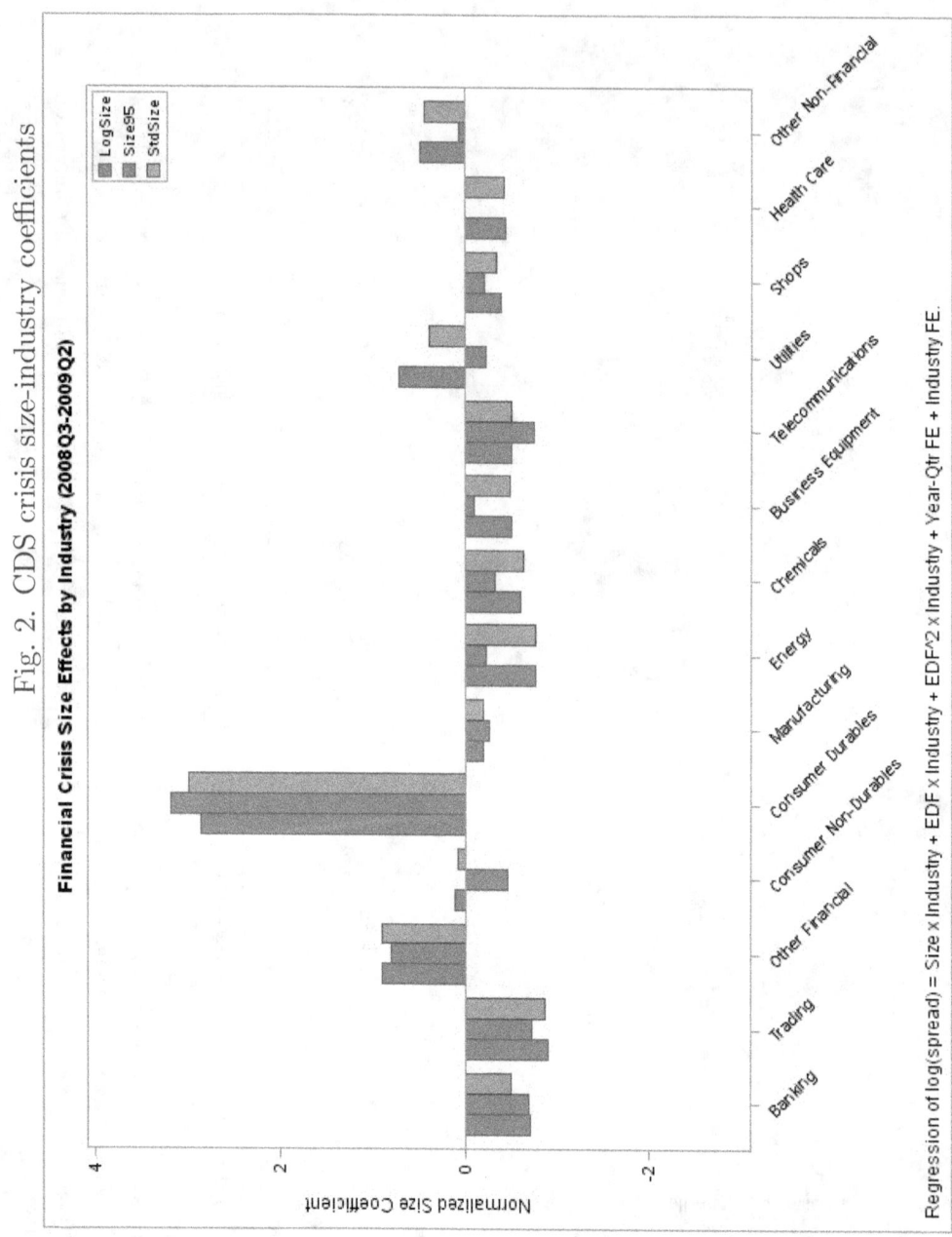

on the size-industry interactions for the CDS crisis subsample for three size variables - log size from Equation 3 (shown in blue), the Size95 indicator from Equation 4 (shown in red), and a standardized size variable (shown in green) which measures the number of standard deviations a firm's size is from the mean log assets of its industry. For ease of comparison, the coefficients are normalized by subtracting the mean value of the coefficients for a given size variable and dividing by the standard deviation of the coefficients. This figure presents coefficients on the size-industry interactions for

Fig. 3. CDS post-crisis size-industry coefficients

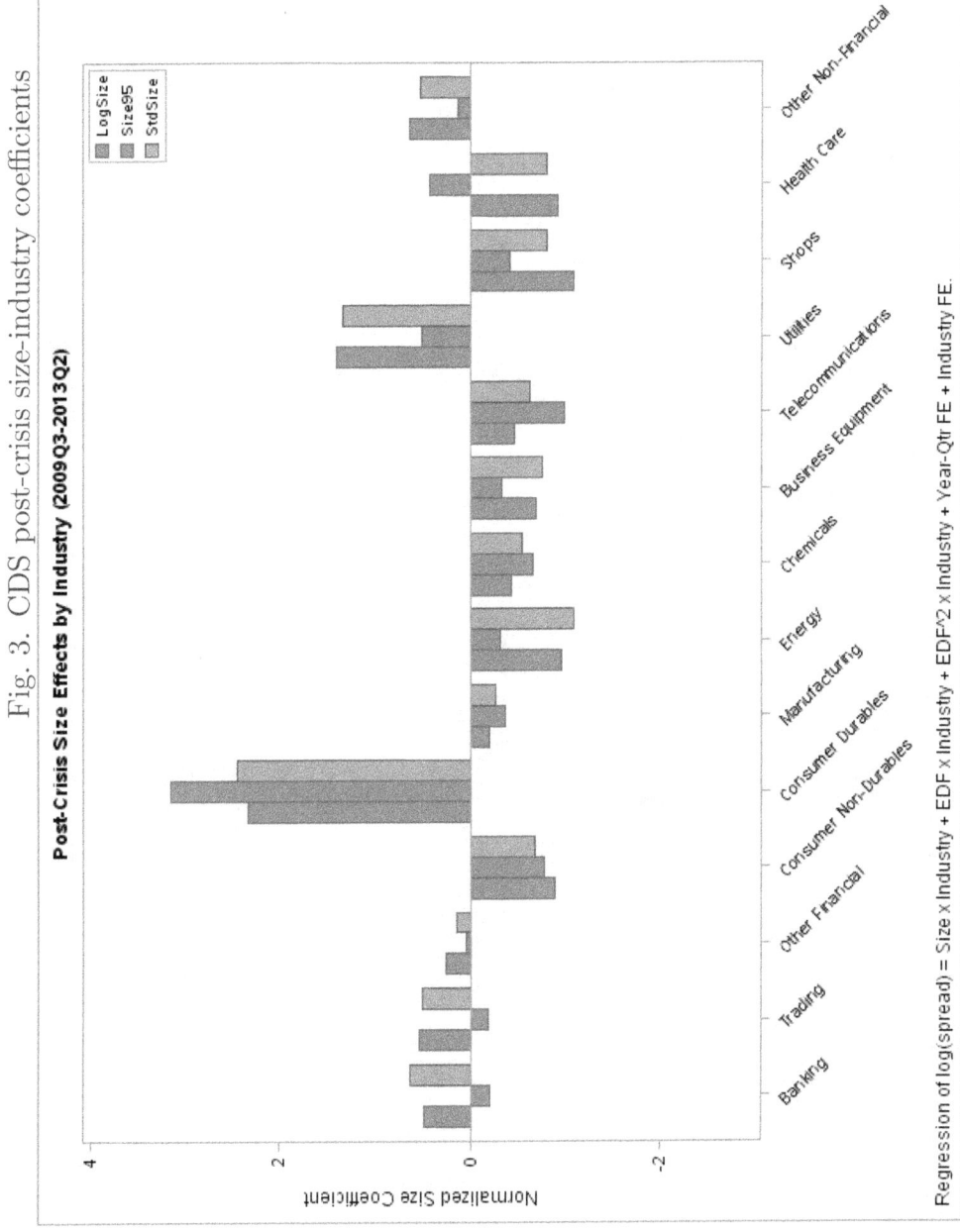

Regression of log(spread) = Size x Industry + EDF x Industry + EDF^2 x Industry + Year-Qtr FE + Industry FE.

the CDS post-crisis subsample for three size variables - log size from Equation 3 (shown in blue), the Size95 indicator from Equation 4 (shown in red), and a standardized size variable (shown in green) which measures the number of standard deviations a firm's size is from the mean log assets of its industry. For ease of comparison, the coefficients are normalized by subtracting the mean value of the coefficients for a given size variable and dividing by the standard deviation of the coefficients. This figure presents coefficients on the size-industry interactions for the bond pre-crisis subsample for

Fig. 4. Bond pre-crisis size-industry coefficients

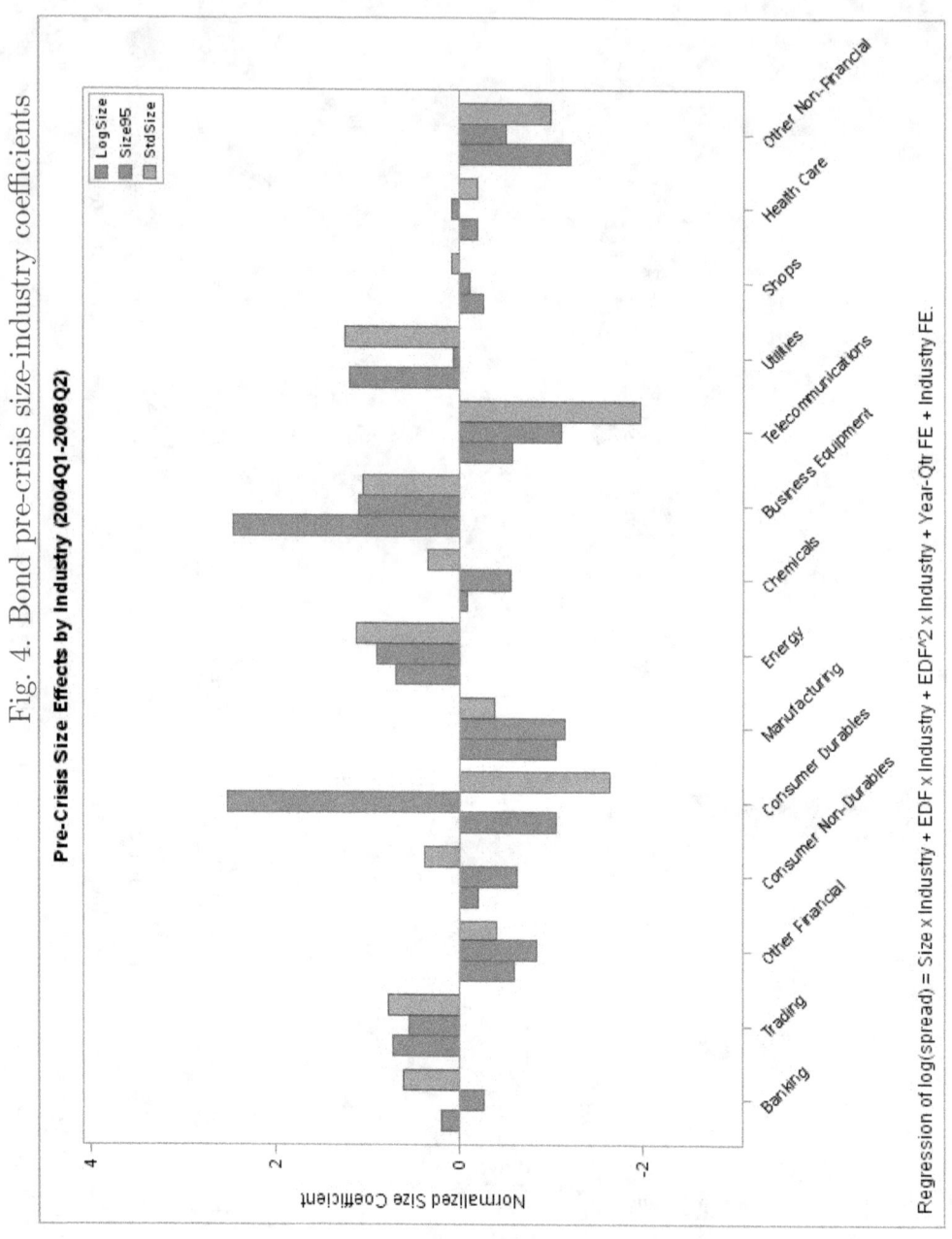

Regression of log(spread) = Size x Industry + EDF x Industry + EDF^2 x Industry + Year-Qtr FE + Industry FE.

three size variables - log size from Equation 3 (shown in blue), the Size95 indicator from Equation 4 (shown in red), and a standardized size variable (shown in green) which measures the number of standard deviations a firm's size is from the mean log assets of its industry. For ease of comparison, the coefficients are normalized by subtracting the mean value of the coefficients for a given size variable and dividing by the standard deviation of the coefficients. This figure presents coefficients on the size-industry interactions for the bond crisis subsample for three size variables - log size from

Fig. 5. Bond crisis size-industry coefficients

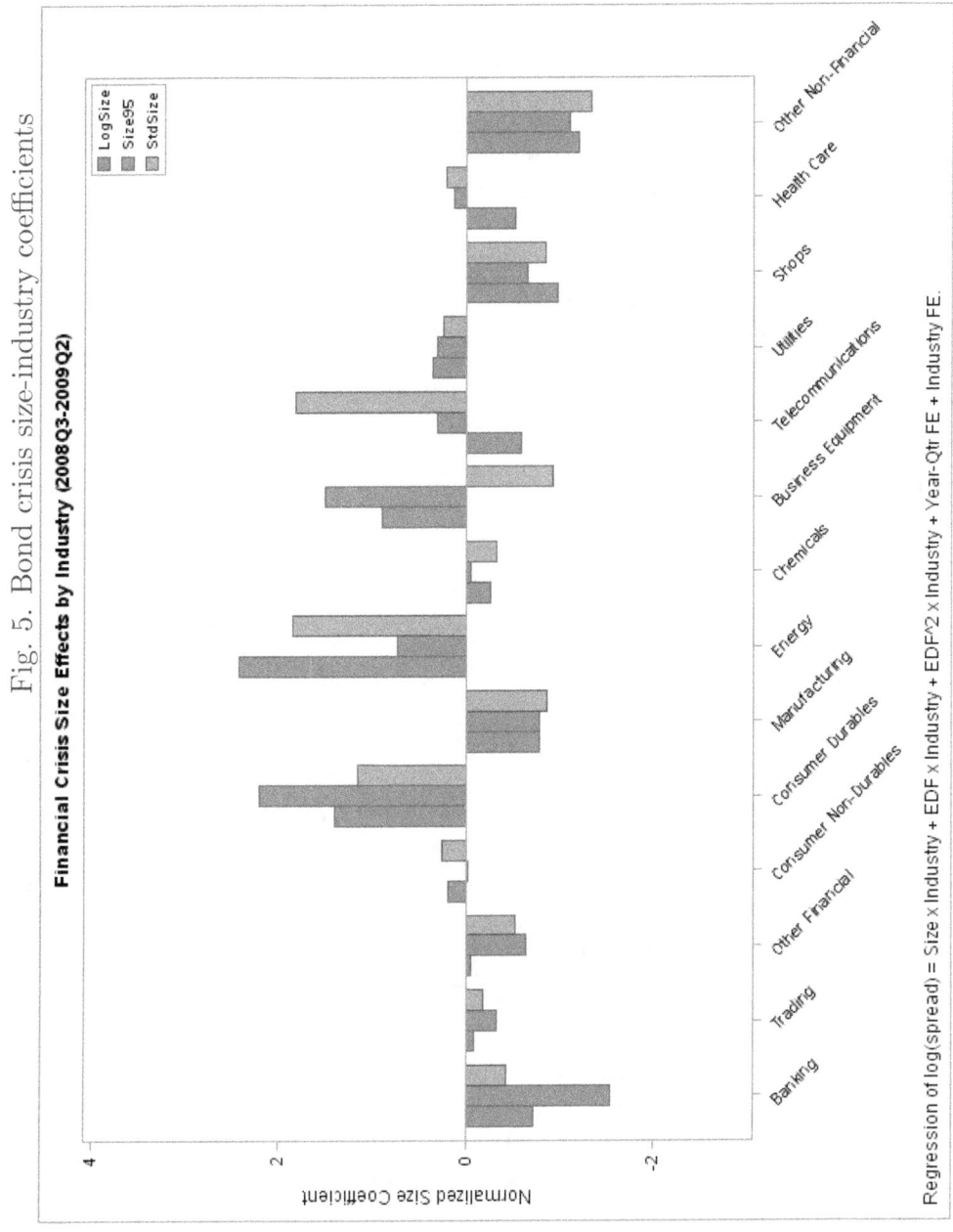

Regression of log(spread) = Size × Industry + EDF × Industry + EDF^2 × Industry + Year-Qtr FE + Industry FE.

Equation 3 (shown in blue), the Size95 indicator from Equation 4 (shown in red), and a standardized size variable (shown in green) which measures the number of standard deviations a firm's size is from the mean log assets of its industry. For ease of comparison, the coefficients are normalized by subtracting the mean value of the coefficients for a given size variable and dividing by the standard deviation of the coefficients. This figure presents

Fig. 6. Bond post-crisis size-industry coefficients

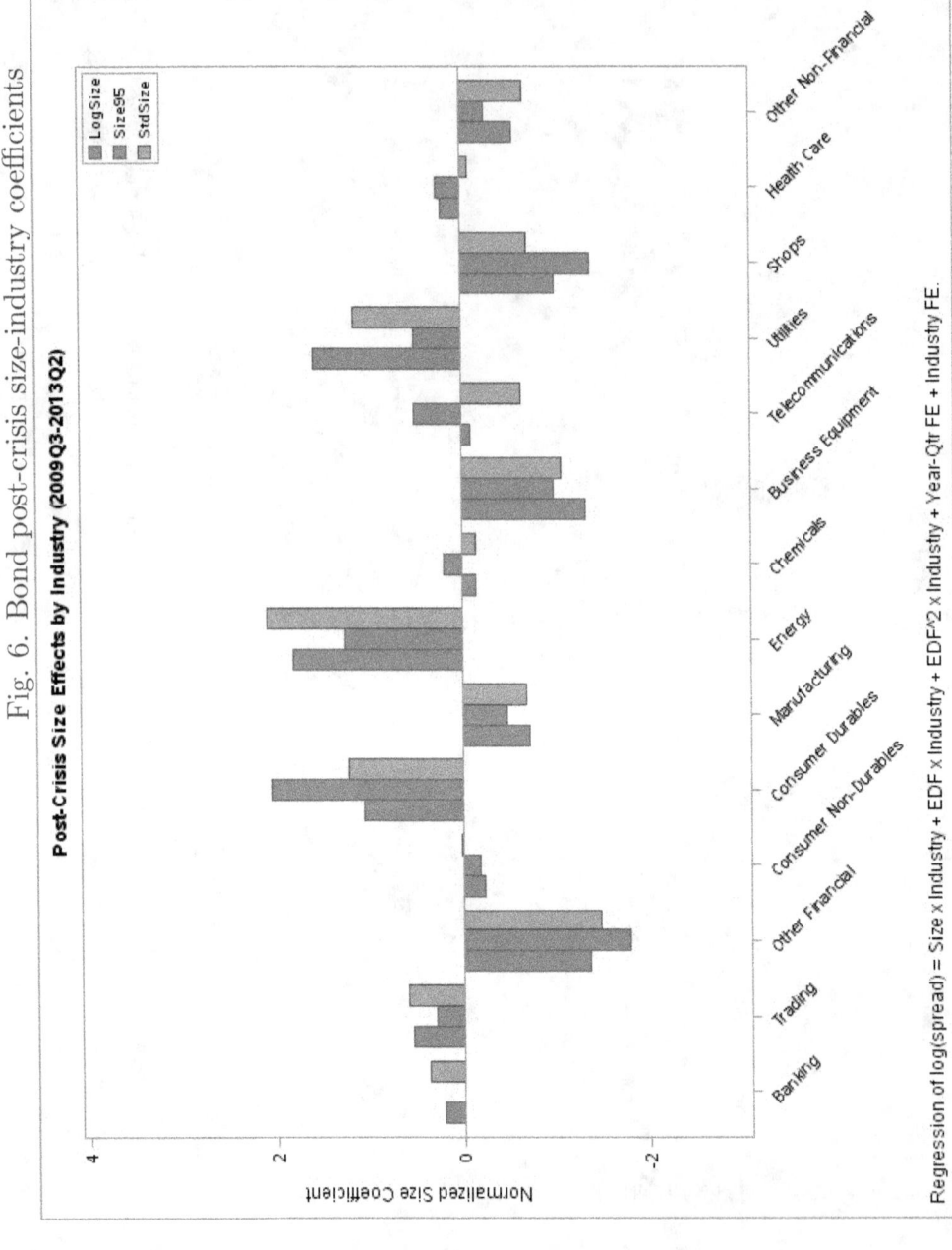

coefficients on the size-industry interactions for the bond post-crisis subsample for three size variables - log size from Equation 3 (shown in blue), the Size95 indicator from Equation 4 (shown in red), and a standardized size variable (shown in green) which measures the number of standard deviations a firm's size is from the mean log assets of its industry. For ease of comparison, the coefficients are normalized by subtracting the mean value of the coefficients for a given size variable and dividing by the standard deviation of the coefficients.

Table 10: **Regression of CDS spread, liquidity controls**

| | (1) Full | (2) Pre-Crisis | (3) Crisis | (4) Post-Crisis |
|---|---|---|---|---|
| LogSize* Banking | -0.024 (**) | -0.004 | -0.028 | -0.025 |
| | (0.012) | (0.006) | (0.050) | (0.021) |
| LogSize* Other Financial | -0.007 | -0.011 (***) | 0.022 | -0.024 (*) |
| | (0.007) | (0.003) | (0.018) | (0.014) |
| LogSize* Trading | -0.018 (***) | -0.012 (***) | -0.059 (***) | -0.021 (***) |
| | (0.005) | (0.004) | (0.015) | (0.006) |
| LogSize* Business Equipment | -0.027 (***) | -0.026 (***) | -0.003 | -0.030 (***) |
| | (0.007) | (0.007) | (0.014) | (0.008) |
| LogSize* Chemicals | -0.026 (***) | -0.025 (***) | -0.022 | -0.019 (**) |
| | (0.008) | (0.007) | (0.015) | (0.008) |
| LogSize* Consumer Durables | 0.077 (***) | 0.057 (***) | 0.175 (*) | 0.064 (***) |
| | (0.018) | (0.018) | (0.090) | (0.017) |
| LogSize* Consumer Non-Durables | -0.027 (*) | -0.007 | 0.003 | -0.039 (*) |
| | (0.014) | (0.009) | (0.037) | (0.022) |
| LogSize* Energy | -0.018 (**) | -0.014 (**) | -0.011 | -0.024 (*) |
| | (0.007) | (0.006) | (0.018) | (0.012) |
| LogSize* Health Care | -0.022 | -0.002 | -0.007 | -0.038 (*) |
| | (0.017) | (0.011) | (0.030) | (0.020) |
| LogSize* Manufacturing | -0.011 (*) | -0.015 (**) | 0.011 | -0.019 (***) |
| | (0.006) | (0.007) | (0.019) | (0.006) |
| LogSize* Other Non-Financial | 0.007 | 0.009 | 0.040 (**) | -0.003 |
| | (0.009) | (0.014) | (0.016) | (0.008) |
| LogSize* Shops | -0.035 (***) | -0.020 (*) | 0.002 | -0.023 |
| | (0.013) | (0.010) | (0.016) | (0.016) |
| LogSize* Telecommunications | -0.007 | 0.011 | -0.013 | -0.048 (***) |
| | (0.012) | (0.017) | (0.019) | (0.015) |
| LogSize* Utilities | 0.007 | 0.002 | 0.007 | 0.001 |
| | (0.006) | (0.006) | (0.016) | (0.007) |
| Adj.$R^2$ | 0.682 | 0.662 | 0.695 | 0.766 |
| N | 14,714 | 7,977 | 1,900 | 4,837 |

This table presents results for estimating Equation 5, which includes controls for liquidity (CDS depth and log of debt issued in past 5 years and CDS depth, interacted across industries) over financial crisis (08Q3-09Q2), pre-crisis (04Q1-08Q2) and post-crisis (09Q3-13Q2) subsamples. All specifications include industry interactions for EDF and $EDF^2$ as well as industry and year-quarter fixed effects. Standard errors are clustered at the firm level. ***, **, and * indicate statistical significance at the 1%, 5% and 10% levels, respectively.

Table 11: **Summary statistics on realized loss given default**

| Industry | # Obs | Mean LGD | Mean Size ($M) |
|---|---|---|---|
| Banking | 4 | 38 | 924 |
| Other Financial | 10 | 58 | 917 |
| Trading | 12 | 63 | 335 |
| Business Equipment | 61 | 58 | 793 |
| Chemicals | 25 | 49 | 1,529 |
| Consumer Durables | 49 | 43 | 1,384 |
| Consumer Non-Durables | 86 | 47 | 657 |
| Energy | 54 | 44 | 541 |
| Health Care | 34 | 54 | 661 |
| Manufacturing | 144 | 48 | 592 |
| Other Non-Financial | 183 | 51 | 820 |
| Shops | 157 | 50 | 448 |
| Telecommunications | 103 | 56 | 2,321 |
| Utilities | 22 | 33 | 2,430 |

Sample consists of all default events from Moody's Default and Recovery Database from April 1987 to April 2013 with an LGD > 0. Loss given default (LGD) is expressed in percentage points. Firm size based on face value of debt outstanding at the time of default.

Table 12: **Coefficient magnitude summary**

| | Full Sample | | | Pre-Crisis | | |
|---|---|---|---|---|---|---|
| | Table 6 | Table 8 | Table 10 | Table 6 | Table 8 | Table 10 |
| Panel A: Full Sample and Pre-crisis | | | | | | |
| LogSize* Banking | -0.2 | -0.2 | -0.2 | -0.0 | -0.1 | -0.0 |
| LogSize* Other Financial | -0.1 | -0.3 | -0.1 | -0.1 | -0.2 | -0.1 |
| LogSize* Trading | -0.2 | -0.1 | -0.2 | -0.1 | -0.0 | -0.1 |
| LogSize* Business Equipment | -0.3 | -0.1 | -0.3 | -0.3 | 0.2 | -0.2 |
| LogSize* Chemicals | -0.3 | -0.2 | -0.2 | -0.3 | -0.1 | -0.2 |
| LogSize* Consumer Durables | 0.6 | 0.0 | 0.7 | 0.6 | -0.2 | 0.5 |
| LogSize* Consumer Non-Durables | -0.3 | -0.2 | -0.3 | -0.1 | -0.1 | -0.1 |
| LogSize* Energy | -0.2 | -0.0 | -0.2 | -0.2 | -0.0 | -0.1 |
| LogSize* Health Care | -0.2 | -0.1 | -0.2 | -0.0 | -0.1 | -0.0 |
| LogSize* Manufacturing | -0.1 | -0.5 | -0.1 | -0.1 | -0.3 | -0.1 |
| LogSize* Other Non-Financial | 0.0 | -0.4 | 0.1 | 0.0 | -0.3 | 0.1 |
| LogSize* Shops | -0.4 | -0.5 | -0.3 | -0.4 | -0.2 | -0.2 |
| LogSize* Telecommunications | -0.1 | -0.2 | -0.1 | -0.0 | -0.2 | 0.1 |
| LogSize* Utilities | 0.0 | 0.1 | 0.1 | 0.0 | 0.0 | 0.0 |
| | | | | | | |
| Panel B: Crisis and Post-crisis | | | | | | |
| LogSize* Banking | -0.5 | -0.5 | -0.3 | -0.2 | -0.2 | -0.2 |
| LogSize* Other Financial | 0.4 | -0.3 | 0.2 | -0.3 | -0.6 | -0.2 |
| LogSize* Trading | -0.3 | -0.3 | -0.6 | -0.2 | -0.1 | -0.2 |
| LogSize* Business Equipment | -0.0 | 0.1 | -0.0 | -0.3 | -0.7 | -0.3 |
| LogSize* Chemicals | -0.1 | -0.3 | -0.2 | -0.2 | -0.3 | -0.2 |
| LogSize* Consumer Durables | 1.9 | 0.3 | 1.7 | 0.2 | 0.1 | 0.6 |
| LogSize* Consumer Non-Durables | 0.0 | -0.2 | 0.0 | -0.4 | -0.3 | -0.4 |
| LogSize* Energy | -0.1 | 0.7 | -0.1 | -0.3 | 0.2 | -0.2 |
| LogSize* Health Care | -0.3 | -0.4 | -0.1 | -0.5 | -0.2 | -0.4 |
| LogSize* Manufacturing | 0.0 | -0.5 | 0.1 | -0.2 | -0.5 | -0.2 |
| LogSize* Other Non-Financial | 0.3 | -0.7 | 0.4 | -0.1 | -0.4 | -0.0 |
| LogSize* Shops | -0.0 | -0.6 | 0.0 | -0.3 | -0.6 | -0.2 |
| LogSize* Telecommunications | -0.0 | -0.4 | -0.1 | -0.3 | -0.3 | -0.5 |
| LogSize* Utilities | 0.2 | -0.1 | 0.1 | 0.0 | 0.3 | 0.0 |

This table summarizes coefficient magnitudes across Tables 6 (regression of log CDS spread), 8 (regression of log bond spread), 10 (CDS spread regression wth liquidity controls). Results represent estimated percent (not percentage point) change in borrowing costs for a 10% increase in size. Pre-crisis period is 2004Q1-2008Q2, financial crisis period is 2008Q3-2009Q2, post-crisis period is 2009Q3-2013Q2.

# Appendix A.   Sample details and additional results

Table A.1: Variable definitions

| | |
|---|---|
| Spread (CDS) | Yield spread (in basis points) between 5-year senior CDS and 5-year treasury bond |
| Spread (Bond) | Yield spread (in basis points) between bond yield to maturity and treasury bond with closest maturity |
| LogSize | Log of book assets (millions) (Compustat: atq) |
| StdSize | Number of standard deviations from the mean of log assets of Compustat firms in the same industry |
| Leverage | Market leverage, 100 * (Debt Principal)/(Debt Principal + Market Cap) (Compustat: (100(dlttq + dlcq) / (cshoq * prccq + dlttq + dlcq)) |
| Depth | Daily number of contributor prices used to calculate the 5-year CDS spread |
| Raise | Sum of new public debt issuance (in Mergent FISD data) over previous 5 years (millions) |
| Size95 | Indicator for size above 95th percentile for Compustat firms in industry |
| Rating | S&P issue-level credit rating ordered from 28 (=AAA) to 1 (=Default) |
| Maturity | Bond issue maturity taken from FISD or SDC |
| EDF | 5-year (CDS) or maturity year (Bond) expected default frequency estimated by Moody's (percentage) |
| LGD | 100 * (1-Realized recovery rate), from Moody's Ultimate Recovery database (percentage) |

Table A.2: **CDS data variable means by period**

| Industry | Spread | EDF | LogSize | StdSize | Leverage | Depth | Raise | Size95 | Rating |
|---|---|---|---|---|---|---|---|---|---|
| Panel A: Full | | | | | | | | | |
| Banking | 178 | 1.53 | 12.1 | 2.1 | 63.6 | 5.9 | 30.0 | 0.5 | 22.3 |
| Other Financial | 269 | 1.58 | 10.6 | 1.2 | 28.9 | 7.2 | 2.6 | 0.2 | 21.5 |
| Trading | 206 | 1.18 | 9.2 | 1.1 | 47.5 | 5.1 | 3.3 | 0.2 | 19.5 |
| Business Equipment | 167 | 0.70 | 9.4 | 1.8 | 18.5 | 5.5 | 4.1 | 0.7 | 19.4 |
| Chemicals | 128 | 0.70 | 9.0 | 1.7 | 20.2 | 6.4 | 5.1 | 0.4 | 21.1 |
| Consumer Durables | 401 | 2.38 | 8.7 | 1.0 | 37.0 | 5.7 | 0.8 | 0.1 | 19.4 |
| Consumer Non-Durables | 202 | 1.04 | 8.8 | 1.2 | 27.8 | 6.5 | 1.8 | 0.2 | 19.7 |
| Energy | 152 | 1.00 | 9.5 | 1.4 | 24.3 | 6.6 | 2.5 | 0.3 | 18.7 |
| Health Care | 164 | 0.50 | 8.8 | 1.7 | 25.9 | 5.8 | 2.4 | 0.6 | 17.6 |
| Manufacturing | 165 | 0.91 | 8.9 | 1.2 | 26.2 | 6.1 | 1.4 | 0.2 | 20.8 |
| Other Non-Financial | 347 | 2.38 | 9.0 | 1.5 | 36.9 | 6.2 | 1.9 | 0.5 | 18.1 |
| Shops | 222 | 1.14 | 9.0 | 1.3 | 27.1 | 7.2 | 2.0 | 0.4 | 18.0 |
| Telecommunications | 302 | 2.04 | 9.5 | 0.9 | 46.5 | 6.0 | 3.9 | 0.2 | 17.1 |
| Utilities | 119 | 0.55 | 9.7 | 0.8 | 46.5 | 5.8 | 1.6 | 0.1 | 20.1 |
| Panel B: Pre-crisis | | | | | | | | | |
| Banking | 71 | 0.36 | 11.9 | 2.1 | 63.0 | 8.1 | 18.2 | 0.6 | 22.5 |
| Other Financial | 75 | 0.37 | 10.6 | 1.2 | 23.7 | 9.6 | 2.0 | 0.2 | 21.7 |
| Trading | 94 | 0.28 | 9.4 | 1.2 | 48.8 | 6.9 | 3.8 | 0.3 | 19.7 |
| Business Equipment | 127 | 0.47 | 9.2 | 1.9 | 15.3 | 6.9 | 5.0 | 0.8 | 19.1 |
| Chemicals | 113 | 0.66 | 8.9 | 1.7 | 19.3 | 8.4 | 4.9 | 0.4 | 20.9 |
| Consumer Durables | 242 | 1.75 | 8.7 | 1.0 | 35.5 | 8.1 | 0.6 | 0.1 | 19.1 |
| Consumer Non-Durables | 120 | 0.32 | 8.8 | 1.2 | 26.0 | 8.4 | 1.4 | 0.2 | 19.8 |
| Energy | 91 | 0.28 | 9.3 | 1.4 | 20.1 | 8.5 | 2.0 | 0.3 | 18.8 |
| Health Care | 124 | 0.29 | 8.6 | 1.8 | 22.0 | 7.7 | 2.3 | 0.6 | 17.6 |
| Manufacturing | 91 | 0.35 | 8.8 | 1.2 | 23.4 | 8.1 | 1.3 | 0.3 | 20.7 |
| Other Non-Financial | 261 | 1.43 | 9.0 | 1.5 | 32.3 | 8.2 | 2.1 | 0.5 | 18.2 |
| Shops | 177 | 0.46 | 8.9 | 1.4 | 23.4 | 9.3 | 1.8 | 0.4 | 18.0 |
| Telecommunications | 283 | 1.75 | 9.4 | 0.9 | 45.1 | 7.4 | 2.5 | 0.2 | 17.1 |
| Utilities | 74 | 0.39 | 9.5 | 0.9 | 45.4 | 7.5 | 1.8 | 0.1 | 19.9 |

Table A.2: **CDS data variable means by period**

| Industry | Spread | EDF | LogSize | StdSize | Leverage | Depth | Raise | Size95 | Rating |
|---|---|---|---|---|---|---|---|---|---|
| Panel C: Crisis | | | | | | | | | |
| Banking | 516 | 3.78 | 12.1 | 2.1 | 72.4 | 5.1 | 49.6 | 0.6 | 22.3 |
| Other Financial | 549 | 3.82 | 10.6 | 1.1 | 40.7 | 6.0 | 3.2 | 0.2 | 21.3 |
| Trading | 619 | 3.18 | 9.0 | 1.1 | 51.4 | 4.3 | 3.1 | 0.2 | 19.3 |
| Business Equipment | 314 | 1.57 | 9.3 | 1.8 | 25.4 | 4.7 | 2.0 | 0.7 | 19.2 |
| Chemicals | 226 | 1.36 | 9.0 | 1.7 | 25.9 | 5.2 | 5.2 | 0.4 | 20.9 |
| Consumer Durables | 1418 | 6.89 | 8.6 | 1.0 | 52.8 | 4.4 | 0.7 | 0.1 | 19.6 |
| Consumer Non-Durables | 371 | 2.35 | 8.8 | 1.1 | 36.1 | 5.7 | 1.7 | 0.2 | 19.5 |
| Energy | 283 | 2.36 | 9.4 | 1.3 | 31.9 | 5.9 | 2.3 | 0.3 | 18.4 |
| Health Care | 264 | 1.39 | 8.7 | 1.6 | 32.1 | 4.8 | 2.2 | 0.5 | 17.4 |
| Manufacturing | 409 | 2.44 | 8.9 | 1.2 | 35.6 | 5.5 | 1.2 | 0.2 | 20.7 |
| Other Non-Financial | 691 | 4.57 | 8.9 | 1.5 | 46.7 | 5.5 | 1.7 | 0.4 | 18.0 |
| Shops | 359 | 2.32 | 9.1 | 1.3 | 35.7 | 6.4 | 2.1 | 0.4 | 18.0 |
| Telecommunications | 449 | 3.59 | 9.3 | 0.9 | 54.5 | 4.9 | 4.0 | 0.2 | 16.5 |
| Utilities | 215 | 0.88 | 9.6 | 0.8 | 52.2 | 5.1 | 1.2 | 0.1 | 20.2 |
| Panel D: Post-crisis | | | | | | | | | |
| Banking | 199 | 2.11 | 12.2 | 2.1 | 62.1 | 4.1 | 41.0 | 0.5 | 22.1 |
| Other Financial | 421 | 2.38 | 10.7 | 1.1 | 32.0 | 4.7 | 3.3 | 0.1 | 21.2 |
| Trading | 213 | 1.57 | 9.2 | 1.0 | 45.0 | 3.6 | 2.7 | 0.2 | 19.3 |
| Business Equipment | 173 | 0.75 | 9.6 | 1.7 | 20.5 | 3.9 | 3.6 | 0.7 | 19.7 |
| Chemicals | 118 | 0.55 | 9.3 | 1.7 | 19.7 | 4.3 | 5.5 | 0.4 | 21.5 |
| Consumer Durables | 288 | 1.80 | 8.7 | 0.9 | 34.3 | 3.5 | 1.0 | 0.1 | 19.8 |
| Consumer Non-Durables | 251 | 1.53 | 8.9 | 1.1 | 27.8 | 4.5 | 2.7 | 0.2 | 19.6 |
| Energy | 181 | 1.39 | 9.8 | 1.3 | 26.8 | 4.6 | 3.3 | 0.3 | 18.8 |
| Health Care | 180 | 0.49 | 9.0 | 1.6 | 28.6 | 4.0 | 2.6 | 0.5 | 17.6 |
| Manufacturing | 185 | 1.14 | 9.1 | 1.2 | 26.8 | 4.0 | 1.7 | 0.2 | 20.8 |
| Other Non-Financial | 347 | 2.80 | 9.0 | 1.5 | 38.9 | 4.2 | 1.8 | 0.5 | 18.1 |
| Shops | 242 | 1.67 | 9.2 | 1.3 | 29.5 | 4.8 | 2.3 | 0.4 | 18.0 |
| Telecommunications | 273 | 1.86 | 9.8 | 0.9 | 45.3 | 4.6 | 6.4 | 0.2 | 17.3 |
| Utilities | 141 | 0.63 | 9.8 | 0.8 | 46.1 | 4.1 | 1.3 | 0.1 | 20.3 |

This table presents CDS sample variable means across full sample (04Q1-13Q2), pre-crisis (04Q1-08Q2), crisis (08Q3-09Q2), and post-crisis (09Q3-13Q2) subsamples. Variables include 5-year CDS spread, expected default probability (EDF), log assets, standardized log assets (measures size in units of standard deviation from the mean of log of assets for Compustat firms in the same industry), market leverage, CDS Depth (a measure of the amount of trading in comparable CDS contracts), sum of debt raised over past 5 years (Raise, $M), an indicator for 95th percentile of size across within-industry Compustat firms, and credit rating (expressed on a 1-28 scale with 28=AAA).

56

Table A.3: **Bond sample variable means by time period**

| Industry | Spread | EDF | LogSize | StdSize | Leverage | Maturity | Size95 | Rating |
|---|---|---|---|---|---|---|---|---|
| Panel A: Full | | | | | | | | |
| Banking | 218 | 1.2 | 13.1 | 2.6 | 70.1 | 6.6 | 0.70 | 22.3 |
| Other Financial | 291 | 1.1 | 10.5 | 1.1 | 29.7 | 9.8 | 0.11 | 19.6 |
| Trading | 166 | 0.8 | 13.0 | 2.4 | 85.5 | 4.2 | 0.79 | 22.6 |
| Business Equipment | 167 | 0.8 | 10.2 | 2.1 | 16.0 | 8.8 | 0.85 | 21.0 |
| Chemicals | 142 | 0.5 | 10.5 | 2.3 | 19.5 | 9.2 | 0.82 | 23.0 |
| Consumer Durables | 628 | 1.4 | 12.0 | 2.0 | 71.5 | 21.2 | 0.89 | 13.5 |
| Consumer Non-Durables | 190 | 0.2 | 9.7 | 1.5 | 24.0 | 9.8 | 0.56 | 20.2 |
| Energy | 227 | 0.6 | 9.9 | 1.6 | 20.7 | 20.0 | 0.73 | 19.5 |
| Health Care | 203 | 0.2 | 8.8 | 1.7 | 14.0 | 10.3 | 0.81 | 20.5 |
| Manufacturing | 202 | 0.8 | 9.9 | 1.6 | 28.4 | 10.5 | 0.65 | 19.8 |
| Other Non-Financial | 334 | 2.3 | 9.8 | 1.8 | 37.9 | 7.3 | 0.74 | 17.7 |
| Shops | 190 | 0.6 | 10.6 | 2.0 | 24.6 | 9.4 | 0.72 | 21.0 |
| Telecommunications | 425 | 10.4 | 9.1 | 1.0 | 44.7 | 3.6 | 0.04 | 15.8 |
| Utilities | 253 | 0.6 | 9.4 | 0.7 | 50.1 | 7.9 | 0.05 | 17.2 |
| Panel B: Pre-crisis | | | | | | | | |
| Banking | 125 | 0.2 | 13.0 | 2.7 | 66.1 | 6.2 | 0.72 | 23.3 |
| Other Financial | 182 | 0.4 | 10.5 | 1.2 | 25.8 | 8.9 | 0.17 | 20.0 |
| Trading | 105 | 0.3 | 12.9 | 2.4 | 86.2 | 4.3 | 0.76 | 23.0 |
| Business Equipment | 175 | 1.2 | 9.6 | 2.0 | 20.9 | 7.3 | 0.75 | 18.2 |
| Chemicals | 102 | 0.6 | 10.2 | 2.2 | 16.5 | 8.4 | 0.78 | 23.3 |
| Consumer Durables | 543 | 1.2 | 12.2 | 2.1 | 71.1 | 23.0 | 0.91 | 14.3 |
| Consumer Non-Durables | 135 | 0.1 | 9.4 | 1.4 | 24.5 | 8.4 | 0.42 | 20.3 |
| Energy | 144 | 0.3 | 9.8 | 1.7 | 18.0 | 15.6 | 0.81 | 19.4 |
| Health Care | 131 | 0.0 | 8.8 | 1.8 | 8.1 | 10.0 | 0.84 | 20.6 |
| Manufacturing | 153 | 0.4 | 9.8 | 1.6 | 27.4 | 10.1 | 0.66 | 19.6 |
| Other Non-Financial | 300 | 3.1 | 9.7 | 1.8 | 38.8 | 7.4 | 0.78 | 17.2 |
| Shops | 149 | 0.2 | 10.2 | 1.9 | 22.3 | 8.4 | 0.72 | 20.4 |
| Telecommunications | 420 | 12.1 | 9.2 | 1.0 | 46.9 | 3.5 | 0.05 | 15.5 |
| Utilities | 159 | 0.2 | 9.5 | 0.8 | 47.0 | 5.8 | 0.07 | 17.3 |
| Panel C: Crisis | | | | | | | | |
| Banking | 600 | 4.6 | 13.2 | 2.7 | 83.4 | 7.0 | 0.69 | 21.9 |
| Other Financial | 687 | 2.4 | 10.5 | 1.1 | 38.4 | 9.9 | 0.09 | 19.5 |
| Trading | 562 | 3.5 | 13.1 | 2.5 | 85.4 | 4.1 | 0.76 | 22.1 |
| Business Equipment | 444 | 1.2 | 10.2 | 2.2 | 20.5 | 8.6 | 0.88 | 20.0 |
| Chemicals | 329 | 0.6 | 10.5 | 2.3 | 27.5 | 9.7 | 0.83 | 22.6 |
| Consumer Durables | 1347 | 2.7 | 12.1 | 2.0 | 84.3 | 22.0 | 0.91 | 10.6 |
| Consumer Non-Durables | 436 | 0.6 | 9.7 | 1.5 | 29.3 | 10.7 | 0.60 | 20.1 |
| Energy | 280 | 0.5 | 10.2 | 1.6 | 17.8 | 14.8 | 0.63 | 20.3 |
| Health Care | 557 | 0.4 | 8.7 | 1.6 | 19.6 | 13.1 | 0.78 | 20.6 |

Table A.3: **Bond sample variable means by time period**

| Industry | Spread | EDF | LogSize | StdSize | Leverage | Maturity | Size95 | Rating |
|---|---|---|---|---|---|---|---|---|
| Manufacturing | 415 | 1.3 | 10.0 | 1.6 | 32.6 | 11.5 | 0.70 | 20.2 |
| Other Non-Financial | 666 | 1.5 | 9.8 | 1.7 | 43.3 | 7.8 | 0.55 | 18.0 |
| Shops | 422 | 1.4 | 10.7 | 2.0 | 28.8 | 10.5 | 0.78 | 21.4 |
| Telecommunications | 698 | 2.1 | 7.8 | 0.9 | 39.4 | 4.4 | 0.00 | 16.1 |
| Utilities | 732 | 1.8 | 9.4 | 0.7 | 65.6 | 11.4 | 0.00 | 15.9 |
| Panel D: Post-crisis | | | | | | | | |
| Banking | 215 | 1.4 | 13.3 | 2.6 | 70.5 | 6.8 | 0.68 | 21.3 |
| Other Financial | 317 | 1.8 | 10.4 | 1.0 | 33.0 | 11.1 | 0.03 | 19.0 |
| Trading | 196 | 1.1 | 13.1 | 2.4 | 83.7 | 3.9 | 0.87 | 21.7 |
| Business Equipment | 97 | 0.3 | 11.1 | 2.3 | 9.1 | 10.7 | 0.99 | 24.3 |
| Chemicals | 142 | 0.3 | 10.9 | 2.3 | 21.9 | 10.5 | 0.90 | 22.7 |
| Consumer Durables | 475 | 1.2 | 11.4 | 1.8 | 67.0 | 15.1 | 0.78 | 12.6 |
| Consumer Non-Durables | 165 | 0.3 | 10.0 | 1.5 | 22.0 | 10.7 | 0.67 | 20.2 |
| Energy | 299 | 0.9 | 10.0 | 1.5 | 24.1 | 25.7 | 0.67 | 19.3 |
| Health Care | 184 | 0.4 | 8.9 | 1.6 | 20.4 | 9.8 | 0.77 | 20.4 |
| Manufacturing | 200 | 1.0 | 10.0 | 1.5 | 28.2 | 10.8 | 0.63 | 19.9 |
| Other Non-Financial | 262 | 0.8 | 10.1 | 1.8 | 33.5 | 6.8 | 0.72 | 18.6 |
| Shops | 177 | 0.9 | 11.0 | 2.1 | 26.2 | 10.3 | 0.71 | 21.7 |
| Telecommunications | 315 | 1.1 | 8.1 | 0.9 | 30.1 | 3.9 | 0.00 | 17.2 |
| Utilities | 295 | 1.2 | 9.0 | 0.4 | 51.3 | 13.3 | 0.00 | 17.6 |

This table presents bond sample variable means across full sample (04Q1-13Q2), pre-crisis (04Q1-08Q2), crisis (08Q3-09Q2), and post-crisis (09Q3-13Q2) subsamples. Variables include 5-year CDS spread, expected default probability (EDF), log assets, standardized log assets (measures size in units of standard deviation from the mean of log of assets for Compustat firms in the same industry), market leverage, maturity in years, an indicator for 95th percentile of size across within-industry Compustat firms, and credit rating (expressed on a 1-28 scale with 28=AAA).

Table A.4: **Regressions of log CDS spread, standardized size variable**

|  | (1) Full | (2) Pre-Crisis | (3) Crisis | (4) Post-Crisis |
|---|---|---|---|---|
| StdSize* Banking | -0.047 (**) | -0.010 | -0.119 | -0.052 (*) |
|  | (0.019) | (0.007) | (0.076) | (0.029) |
| StdSize* Other Financial | -0.048 (**) | -0.029 (***) | 0.119 (**) | -0.110 (***) |
|  | (0.022) | (0.008) | (0.048) | (0.040) |
| StdSize* Trading | -0.045 (***) | -0.037 (***) | -0.096 (**) | -0.048 (***) |
|  | (0.011) | (0.008) | (0.039) | (0.018) |
| StdSize* Business Equipment | -0.076 (***) | -0.083 (***) | -0.003 | -0.076 (***) |
|  | (0.017) | (0.017) | (0.033) | (0.024) |
| StdSize* Chemicals | -0.076 (***) | -0.079 (***) | -0.036 | -0.061 (***) |
|  | (0.019) | (0.017) | (0.030) | (0.018) |
| StdSize* Consumer Durables | 0.210 (***) | 0.182 (***) | 0.636 (***) | 0.078 |
|  | (0.058) | (0.048) | (0.201) | (0.050) |
| StdSize* Consumer Non-Durables | -0.085 (**) | -0.024 | 0.008 | -0.099 (***) |
|  | (0.033) | (0.026) | (0.081) | (0.034) |
| StdSize* Energy | -0.072 (***) | -0.060 (***) | -0.038 | -0.082 (**) |
|  | (0.021) | (0.016) | (0.041) | (0.033) |
| StdSize* Health Care | -0.057 | -0.014 | -0.076 | -0.135 (**) |
|  | (0.047) | (0.024) | (0.078) | (0.062) |
| StdSize* Manufacturing | -0.033 (**) | -0.034 (***) | 0.008 | -0.047 (***) |
|  | (0.014) | (0.013) | (0.040) | (0.016) |
| StdSize* Other Non-Financial | 0.012 | 0.010 | 0.108 (***) | -0.019 |
|  | (0.022) | (0.031) | (0.038) | (0.024) |
| StdSize* Shops | -0.102 (***) | -0.107 (***) | -0.003 | -0.074 (**) |
|  | (0.032) | (0.040) | (0.040) | (0.033) |
| StdSize* Telecommunications | -0.027 | -0.015 | -0.008 | -0.088 (**) |
|  | (0.035) | (0.039) | (0.040) | (0.044) |
| StdSize* Utilities | 0.003 | 0.002 | 0.025 | 0.006 |
|  | (0.010) | (0.009) | (0.026) | (0.013) |
| Adj.$R^2$ | 0.664 | 0.646 | 0.674 | 0.718 |
| N | 17,486 | 8,227 | 1,984 | 7,275 |

This table presents results of estimating Equation 3 using a standardized size measure (which expresses size in terms of standard deviations from the mean of log assets by industry) across financial crisis (2008Q3-2009Q2), pre-crisis (2004Q1-2008Q2) and post-crisis (2009Q3-2013Q2) subsamples. All specifications include industry interactions for EDF and $EDF^2$ as well as industry and year-quarter fixed effects. Standard errors are clustered at the firm level. ***, **, and * indicate statistical significance at the 1%, 5% and 10% levels, respectively.

Table A.5: **Regressions of log bond spread, standardized size variable**

| | (1) Full | (2) Pre-Crisis | (3) Crisis | (4) Post-Crisis |
|---|---|---|---|---|
| StdSize* Banking | -0.045 (***) | -0.021 (***) | -0.104 (***) | -0.043 (**) |
| | (0.011) | (0.005) | (0.037) | (0.019) |
| StdSize* Other Financial | -0.108 (***) | -0.056 (***) | -0.131 (*) | -0.204 (***) |
| | (0.032) | (0.020) | (0.067) | (0.066) |
| StdSize* Trading | -0.023 | -0.014 (*) | -0.072 | -0.020 |
| | (0.022) | (0.008) | (0.070) | (0.030) |
| StdSize* Business Equipment | -0.048 | -0.006 | -0.166 (***) | -0.183 (***) |
| | (0.055) | (0.067) | (0.052) | (0.024) |
| StdSize* Chemicals | -0.050 (*) | -0.030 | -0.096 (**) | -0.093 (*) |
| | (0.028) | (0.026) | (0.044) | (0.054) |
| StdSize* Consumer Durables | 0.008 | -0.111 | 0.112 | 0.027 |
| | (0.107) | (0.104) | (0.151) | (0.097) |
| StdSize* Consumer Non-Durables | -0.049 | -0.031 | -0.014 | -0.074 |
| | (0.047) | (0.034) | (0.090) | (0.048) |
| StdSize* Energy | 0.026 | -0.001 | 0.178 (*) | 0.065 |
| | (0.049) | (0.024) | (0.106) | (0.071) |
| StdSize* Health Care | 0.053 | -0.029 (*) | -0.022 | -0.094 (***) |
| | (0.033) | (0.016) | (0.144) | (0.032) |
| StdSize* Manufacturing | -0.134 (***) | -0.069 (***) | -0.151 (***) | -0.149 (***) |
| | (0.031) | (0.022) | (0.053) | (0.033) |
| StdSize* Other Non-Financial | -0.121 (***) | -0.086 (***) | -0.221 (***) | -0.140 (***) |
| | (0.019) | (0.021) | (0.043) | (0.024) |
| StdSize* Shops | -0.115 (***) | -0.043 (***) | -0.160 (***) | -0.143 (***) |
| | (0.019) | (0.015) | (0.036) | (0.026) |
| StdSize* Telecommunications | -0.098 (***) | -0.126 (***) | 0.195 (**) | -0.133 (***) |
| | (0.027) | (0.035) | (0.078) | (0.047) |
| StdSize* Utilities | 0.010 | 0.004 | -0.016 | 0.034 |
| | (0.014) | (0.013) | (0.036) | (0.065) |
| Maturity | 0.001 (***) | 0.001 (***) | -0.001 (**) | 0.001 (***) |
| | (0.000) | (0.000) | (0.001) | (0.000) |
| Adj.$R^2$ | 0.688 | 0.661 | 0.625 | 0.682 |
| N | 15,466 | 7,892 | 1,766 | 5,808 |

This table presents results of estimating Equation 3 using a standardized size measure (which expresses size in terms of standard deviations from the mean of log assets by industry) across financial crisis (2008Q3-2009Q2), pre-crisis (2004Q1-2008Q2) and post-crisis (2009Q3-2013Q2) subsamples. All specifications control for maturity and include industry interactions for EDF and $EDF^2$ as well as industry and year-quarter fixed effects. Standard errors are clustered at the firm level. ***, **, and * indicate statistical significance at the 1%, 5% and 10% levels, respectively.

Table A.6: **Regressions of log CDS spread, matched CDS-TRACE sample**

|  | (1) Full | (2) Pre-Crisis | (3) Crisis | (4) Post-Crisis |
|---|---|---|---|---|
| LogSize* Banking | -0.014 (***) | -0.004 | -0.027 | -0.017 (**) |
|  | (0.005) | (0.003) | (0.021) | (0.008) |
| LogSize* Other Financial | -0.012 | -0.009 (***) | 0.039 (***) | -0.034 (**) |
|  | (0.008) | (0.002) | (0.015) | (0.017) |
| LogSize* Trading | -0.019 (***) | -0.013 (***) | -0.046 (***) | -0.016 (**) |
|  | (0.005) | (0.004) | (0.015) | (0.007) |
| LogSize* Business Equipment | -0.035 (***) | -0.041 (***) | -0.009 | -0.024 (***) |
|  | (0.006) | (0.008) | (0.015) | (0.006) |
| LogSize* Chemicals | -0.029 (***) | -0.034 (***) | -0.013 | -0.019 (***) |
|  | (0.008) | (0.007) | (0.012) | (0.007) |
| LogSize* Consumer Durables | 0.079 (***) | 0.068 (***) | 0.224 (***) | 0.038 (***) |
|  | (0.010) | (0.010) | (0.033) | (0.012) |
| LogSize* Consumer Non-Durables | -0.027 (*) | -0.008 | 0.016 | -0.035 (*) |
|  | (0.014) | (0.010) | (0.032) | (0.018) |
| LogSize* Energy | -0.023 (***) | -0.027 (***) | -0.015 | -0.019 |
|  | (0.009) | (0.008) | (0.016) | (0.014) |
| LogSize* Health Care | -0.026 | -0.006 | -0.027 | -0.052 (**) |
|  | (0.019) | (0.010) | (0.029) | (0.022) |
| LogSize* Manufacturing | -0.015 (**) | -0.019 (***) | -0.002 | -0.018 (***) |
|  | (0.006) | (0.006) | (0.017) | (0.006) |
| LogSize* Other Non-Financial | -0.003 | -0.005 | 0.020 | -0.006 |
|  | (0.006) | (0.009) | (0.013) | (0.007) |
| LogSize* Shops | -0.033 (***) | -0.022 (**) | -0.002 | -0.027 |
|  | (0.010) | (0.009) | (0.019) | (0.017) |
| LogSize* Telecommunications | -0.010 | -0.000 | -0.004 | -0.021 |
|  | (0.014) | (0.019) | (0.019) | (0.015) |
| LogSize* Utilities | 0.002 | 0.003 | -0.005 | 0.003 |
|  | (0.007) | (0.008) | (0.019) | (0.009) |
| Adj.$R^2$ | 0.671 | 0.670 | 0.696 | 0.722 |
| N | 12,812 | 5,658 | 1,547 | 5,607 |

This table illustrates results analogous to those in Table 6 but using a sample of CDS issues matched with bond data in TRACE. All specifications include industry interactions for EDF and $EDF^2$ as well as industry and year-quarter fixed effects. Standard errors are clustered at the firm level. ***, **, and * indicate statistical significance at the 1%, 5% and 10% levels, respectively.

Table A.7: **Regressions of log CDS spread, leverage and rating controls**

|  | (1) Full | (2) Pre-Crisis | (3) Crisis | (4) Post-Crisis |
|---|---|---|---|---|
| LogSize* Banking | -0.040 (***) | -0.017 (***) | -0.126 (***) | -0.044 (***) |
|  | (0.004) | (0.003) | (0.013) | (0.009) |
| LogSize* Other Financial | -0.042 (***) | -0.020 (***) | -0.027 | -0.074 (***) |
|  | (0.012) | (0.007) | (0.020) | (0.019) |
| LogSize* Trading | -0.026 (***) | -0.005 | -0.050 (***) | -0.024 (**) |
|  | (0.008) | (0.006) | (0.018) | (0.010) |
| LogSize* Business Equipment | -0.025 | -0.021 | -0.005 | -0.032 (**) |
|  | (0.017) | (0.015) | (0.038) | (0.016) |
| LogSize* Chemicals | -0.019 (**) | 0.002 | 0.005 | -0.037 (***) |
|  | (0.009) | (0.011) | (0.024) | (0.013) |
| LogSize* Consumer Durables | -0.064 (***) | -0.032 (*) | -0.033 | -0.071 (***) |
|  | (0.025) | (0.018) | (0.064) | (0.015) |
| LogSize* Consumer Non-Durables | -0.007 | -0.008 | 0.048 | -0.015 |
|  | (0.016) | (0.013) | (0.040) | (0.021) |
| LogSize* Energy | -0.020 (**) | -0.024 (***) | -0.013 | -0.023 (**) |
|  | (0.008) | (0.008) | (0.018) | (0.011) |
| LogSize* Health Care | -0.013 | 0.001 | 0.015 | -0.024 |
|  | (0.019) | (0.019) | (0.034) | (0.019) |
| LogSize* Manufacturing | -0.024 (***) | -0.016 (***) | -0.007 | -0.034 (***) |
|  | (0.009) | (0.006) | (0.020) | (0.012) |
| LogSize* Other Non-Financial | -0.022 | -0.020 | -0.012 | -0.026 |
|  | (0.014) | (0.014) | (0.029) | (0.017) |
| LogSize* Shops | -0.030 (***) | -0.030 (***) | -0.002 | -0.036 (**) |
|  | (0.011) | (0.009) | (0.030) | (0.015) |
| LogSize* Telecommunications | 0.009 | 0.026 | 0.018 | -0.019 |
|  | (0.017) | (0.023) | (0.023) | (0.015) |
| LogSize* Utilities | -0.004 | -0.000 | -0.002 | -0.018 |
|  | (0.008) | (0.008) | (0.017) | (0.013) |
| Adj.$R^2$ | 0.560 | 0.570 | 0.577 | 0.573 |
| N | 16,006 | 7,508 | 1,804 | 6,694 |

This table presents results for estimating an equation based on Equation 3 but including controls for leverage and credit rating, interacted across industries, over financial crisis (08Q3-09Q2), pre-crisis (04Q1-08Q2) and post-crisis (09Q3-13Q2) subsamples. All specifications include industry interactions for EDF and $EDF^2$ as well as industry and year-quarter fixed effects. Standard errors are clustered at the firm level. ***, **, and * indicate statistical significance at the 1%, 5% and 10% levels, respectively.

Table A.8: **Regressions of log bond spread, leverage and rating controls**

| | (1) Full | (2) Pre-Crisis | (3) Crisis | (4) Post-Crisis |
|---|---|---|---|---|
| LogSize* Banking | -0.021 (***) | -0.007 | -0.076 (***) | -0.029 (**) |
| | (0.005) | (0.007) | (0.014) | (0.013) |
| LogSize* Other Financial | -0.013 | -0.006 | -0.022 | -0.026 (*) |
| | (0.008) | (0.007) | (0.019) | (0.014) |
| LogSize* Trading | 0.002 | 0.004 | -0.350 (***) | -0.049 |
| | (0.013) | (0.013) | (0.047) | (0.032) |
| LogSize* Business Equipment | -0.049 (***) | -0.033 (**) | -0.079 | -0.067 (***) |
| | (0.017) | (0.016) | (0.054) | (0.013) |
| LogSize* Chemicals | -0.014 | -0.008 | -0.051 (**) | -0.024 |
| | (0.012) | (0.010) | (0.020) | (0.018) |
| LogSize* Consumer Durables | -0.089 (***) | -0.169 | -0.432 (***) | -0.067 (***) |
| | (0.029) | (0.157) | (0.155) | (0.017) |
| LogSize* Consumer Non-Durables | -0.000 | 0.006 | 0.036 | -0.017 (***) |
| | (0.007) | (0.004) | (0.024) | (0.003) |
| LogSize* Energy | 0.011 | -0.011 | 0.035 | 0.003 |
| | (0.008) | (0.009) | (0.033) | (0.032) |
| LogSize* Health Care | -0.022 | -0.006 | -0.158 (***) | -0.052 |
| | (0.035) | (0.009) | (0.035) | (0.048) |
| LogSize* Manufacturing | -0.029 (**) | -0.035 (***) | -0.027 | -0.008 |
| | (0.014) | (0.013) | (0.027) | (0.018) |
| LogSize* Other Non-Financial | -0.024 | -0.011 | -0.071 (***) | -0.069 (***) |
| | (0.016) | (0.017) | (0.018) | (0.022) |
| LogSize* Shops | -0.019 (*) | -0.001 | -0.009 | -0.012 |
| | (0.010) | (0.009) | (0.010) | (0.029) |
| LogSize* Telecommunications | -0.015 | -0.007 | -0.112 (***) | -0.007 (***) |
| | (0.009) | (0.011) | (0.010) | (0.002) |
| LogSize* Utilities | -0.022 (*) | -0.010 (*) | 0.026 | -0.045 |
| | (0.012) | (0.005) | (0.058) | (0.071) |
| Maturity | 0.001 (***) | 0.002 (***) | -0.001 | 0.001 (***) |
| | (0.000) | (0.000) | (0.001) | (0.000) |
| Adj.$R^2$ | 0.687 | 0.613 | 0.700 | 0.704 |
| N | 14,376 | 7,057 | 1,679 | 5,640 |

This table presents results for estimating an equation based on Equation 3 using bond yield spreads from TRACE but including controls for leverage and credit rating, interacted across industries, over the financial crisis (08Q3-09Q2), pre-crisis (04Q1-08Q2) and post-crisis (09Q3-13Q2) subsamples. All specifications control for maturity and include industry interactions for EDF and $EDF^2$ as well as industry and year-quarter fixed effects. Standard errors are clustered at the firm level. ***, **, and * indicate statistical significance at the 1%, 5% and 10% levels, respectively.

Table A.9: **Regressions of LGD on log size**

| Variable | (1) No FE | (2) Year FE | (3) Year, Ind FE | (4) FE+Size*Indus |
|---|---|---|---|---|
| LogSize | -2.747 (***) | -2.562 (***) | -2.730 (***) | |
| | (0.713) | (0.715) | (0.733) | |
| LogSize* Banking | | | | 5.252 |
| | | | | (8.881) |
| LogSize* Other Financial | | | | -7.593 |
| | | | | (5.518) |
| LogSize* Trading | | | | -2.608 |
| | | | | (7.668) |
| LogSize* Business Equipment | | | | -6.058 (***) |
| | | | | (2.286) |
| LogSize* Chemicals | | | | -5.416 |
| | | | | (3.388) |
| LogSize* Consumer Durables | | | | -7.292 (***) |
| | | | | (1.870) |
| LogSize* Consumer Non-Durables | | | | -0.179 |
| | | | | (2.576) |
| LogSize* Energy | | | | -4.373 |
| | | | | (4.018) |
| LogSize* Health Care | | | | -3.448 |
| | | | | (2.723) |
| LogSize* Manufacturing | | | | -0.984 |
| | | | | (2.058) |
| LogSize* Other Non-Financial | | | | -5.166 (***) |
| | | | | (1.469) |
| LogSize* Shops | | | | 0.649 |
| | | | | (2.173) |
| LogSize* Telecommunications | | | | 0.784 |
| | | | | (2.003) |
| LogSize* Utilities | | | | -3.554 |
| | | | | (3.105) |
| N | 944 | 944 | 944 | 944 |
| $R^2$ | 0.017 | 0.122 | 0.149 | 0.166 |

This table presents regressions of realized LGD on log size (Columns 1-3) and realized LGD on log size-industry interactions (Column 4) using default and recovery data from Moody's Ultimate Recovery Database with LGD $> 0$. LGD is measured in percentage points; LogSize is the log of the face value of debt outstanding at the time of default. *** indicates statistical significance at the 1% level.